HOW TO
HIRE AND
MOTIVATE
MANUFACTURERS'
REPRESENTATIVES

HOW TO HIRE AND MOTIVATE MANUFACTURERS' REPRESENTATIVES

William H. Krause

amacom A Division of
American Management Associations

Library of Congress Cataloging in Publication Data

Krause, William H
   How to hire and motivate manufacturers' representatives.

   Includes index.
   1. Manufacturers' agents.   2. Sales management.
  3. Sales personnel—Recruiting.   I. Title.
HF5420.K7   658.31′1   76-18944
ISBN 0-8144-5386-4
ISBN 0-8144-7518-3 pbk

First AMACOM paperback edition 1979.

For Dave Braack

good friend and partner
through the lean and good years

PREFACE

As a manufacturers' representative whose sales agency represents seven companies, I have seven sales managers, all of whom have one thing in common: they want our agency to sell as much as possible of their product in Texas, Oklahoma, and the surrounding areas. And that's where the similarity ends. Each sales manager and the firm he works for have different policies and procedures for hiring and motivating their manufacturers' representatives. Some are very successful and several are considerably less so. These differences are what this book is all about.

From the experiences I've had with the successful firms, and through my association with my fellow representatives, I've discovered the practices that work in hiring and motivating professional reps. I'm also extremely well acquainted with the practices that don't work. By presenting the techniques that successful firms employ, as simply and forthright as possible, I hope to help the veteran sales manager, already marketing through manufacturers' reps, improve his batting average. If, as a result of one hint he gets from this book, he improves his company's sales by just 10 percent, he can easily assess the value received.

I hope also to guide the sales manager whose firm is just beginning to use manufacturers' representatives through the maze of conflicting theories of sales administration. I'll present a positive program that he can follow right from the beginning.

Finally, I hope this book will encourage standardization of many of the sales management functions within companies that use this mode of selling. That alone would create a healthy, productive relationship between the professional manufacturers' representatives and the companies (principals) they represent.

Some companies, through either sheer neglect or inability to grasp the basic principles of good sales management of their manufacturers' representative programs, will continue to obtain disappointing results. Others are learning from their mistakes and are improving. Still others (few in number) have reached the professional stage in the motivation of their manufacturers' representatives and are reaping the rewards of good, profitable sales increases each year. The variations in sales management that the manufacturers' representative is subjected to prevent him from realizing his full potential as a salesman. He recognizes this, and in an effort to maintain high effectiveness he tends to work harder for a company that, by understanding and fulfilling his needs, makes his job easier and more rewarding both financially and psychologically.

I've purposely stayed away from the clinical, detailed approach of the more common procedures used in sales management. There are on the bookshelves many authoritative volumes that cover the technical expertise needed for conducting a productive sales program. The key lies in applying the correct interpretation to these techniques when working with manufacturers' representatives. Take sales meetings, for instance. The general rules apply—organization is important, location is important, and timing is important. But these three elements, as you'll discover, must often be planned quite differently from the way you'd plan a meeting for sales people who are direct employees of your company.

These two groups, the manufacturers' representatives and the direct-employee salesmen, possess widely separate characteristics, and it's seldom that hiring and motivational techniques developed for one group will work with the other. By knowing and recognizing these differences, you'll be able to conduct a more intelligent campaign in recruiting and directing a corps of professional manufacturers' representatives.

Your task will not be a simple one, for the truth is that there are too few *professional* manufacturers' representatives in business today, and it's the professional who'll help you the most. He is the man you should seek out with every means possible. Finding, hiring, and motivating him is a tough job, but if you dedicate yourself and your company to an enlightened sales representative program as outlined here, the rewards will be great in terms of sales and profits.

While nepotism is deplored as a deterrent to initiative and progress, I find it works very well when writing a book. My oldest son, Scott, an English scholar, was of immeasurable aid in editing my efforts for clarity and grammatical correctness. My middle son, Kenneth, an entrepreneur in his own right, added helpful comments on some of my basic philosophy; and Barry, the youngest of the three, applied his mathematical skills in compiling the RepSurvey results to which reference is made throughout the book.

I also now understand why so many authors thank their wives for their understanding and help with the manuscript. Joyce cheerfully pounded away at the electric upon my slightest whim for a revision or rewrite and completed the final manuscript ahead of schedule. My thanks to my family for their encouragement and assistance.

William H. Krause

CONTENTS

Part One

FINDING AND
HIRING
THE PROFESSIONALS

1

MARKETING THROUGH MANUFACTURERS' REPRESENTATIVES

History, theory, and the real-life payoff

Billions of dollars worth of goods have been sold through manufacturers' representatives during this century, yet there's little historical documentation of how this prominent method of selling got its start. We do know, however, that over the years there's been little change in the basic overall function of the manufacturers' representative or in the general ground rules governing the arrangements between the rep and the companies he represents.

A Child of Opportunity

A manufacturers' representative may be defined as a man or a firm who sells the products of one or several companies in an exclusive territory, and whose only remuneration is a predetermined commission received from the company based on the dollar value of sales in that territory. The manufacturers' rep pays all his selling and office expenses out of his commissions.

Manufacturers' representative firms may be one-man or multi-man operations. They may be known as manufacturers' agents, sales agents, sales representatives, or just plain "reps." For the sake of brevity we will use the term "sales rep," or simply "rep," throughout

3

this book to denote the manufacturers' representative firm, one-man or multi-man.

Probably the earliest users of reps, dating back to the last century, were railway supply firms. All railways used similar products, and their headquarters were in many of the major cities across the nation. This commonality of need required a national selling program by the firms making wheels, axles, and all the other replacement parts used on freight and passenger cars as well as locomotives.

Since, in those days, it would take months for a sales manager to visit these widely separated buying offices, the railway supply firms appointed commissioned men in the key cities. As the country's industrial growth accelerated, so did the number of railways and the accompanying rolling stock to carry the manufactured goods to the far reaches of the nation.

Gradually, companies with less well defined marketing targets realized that they could expand their sales nationally without a large expenditure in direct sales costs by using representatives to supplement their local or regional sales network. But many companies remained unaware of this style of selling, and others, that *were* aware of manufacturers' representatives, remained somewhat suspicious of men who made their living on a strictly commission basis. This prejudice prevented them from taking advantage of the national market that was ready and waiting for their products.

At one time there was a certain justification for this attitude. Years ago the rep was often considered a necessary evil by his principals. His ethics were not always simon pure and his selling tactics were often unorthodox. He obtained much of his business through close friendships with the owner or purchasing agent of his customer's firm. Often he lived exclusively from the commissions earned on one or two major accounts. Dealings with these accounts were jealously guarded from the companies he represented. Most correspondence and communications were routed through him. He had little product knowledge and was completely uninterested in learning the technical aspects of the products he sold.

In those days purchasing departments, with a few notable exceptions, were a depository for employees who could not qualify for positions in other departments—needy relatives of the owner, executives who were no longer in favor, or loyal employees getting ready for retirement. Their purchasing functions consisted in writing up orders for favored vendors, or phoning a salesman at a local industrial supply house and having him handle the details. Competitive bids were taken only so the favored supplier would know what price to submit, perhaps a little higher than the lowest bidder but sufficiently attractive to receive the order.

These practices changed rather rapidly in the years after World War II. Managements, prodded by their cost accountants who had finally learned of the cost savings offered by intelligent buying practices, set out on pilgrimages to find their purchasing departments, usually located in some remote portion of the plant previously condemned by the local building inspector. When they found the elusive department, they'd meet with the purchasing people to enlighten them about their new importance to the company. They explained how vital the efficient functioning of the purchasing department was to the firm's overall financial health.

Except for an occasional misplaced genius, the purchasing personnel were incapable of rising to this new challenge, and out of their ruins rose a new breed of professional buyers. These were men who knew efficient buying practices, who had been schooled in purchasing classes at leading universities, and who had attended seminars on purchasing conducted by business-related groups.

Imagine the shock of our old-time back-slapping rep on his first encounter with the new purchasing man, his bewilderment at being told that his principal's performance had been assessed by modern measurement systems and was found lacking in quality, delivery, and end-use cost. But don't underestimate the tenacity and versatility of the rep. After all, he had been successful through his ability to give his customers what they wanted, whether it was a free lunch or overnight delivery of a critical component.

The good rep responded to this new competitive climate by taking a more active interest in his principals' product lines and by familiarizing himself with the technical aspects of the products he sold. At the same time he recognized that his own selling philosophy would have to undergo uncomfortable changes. No longer could he rely strictly on his friendship with the purchasing agent. His friend in purchasing, if he was still there, was under increasing pressure to buy intelligently. If the rep felt it was too late to change his own techniques, he'd often bring in younger blood to help him cope with the new purchasing people. He joined MANA (Manufacturers' Agents National Association), an association of reps formed to help the individual rep become a reliable sales professional.

Out of all this came a new image of the manufacturers' representative, an image of a truly modern man or agency who would do a first-class job of selling for his principals.

As reps became more adept at their trade and as their results improved, old prejudices against them were broken down. Many companies with aggressive managements began to look seriously at markets outside their local or regional area. They knew that producers of similar products may have costs that vary widely. An efficient machine tool, a knowledgeable production manager, or a secret, inexpensive source of raw material can readily give one company a competitive price advantage over another. These companies knew that this occurred in their present selling locale and reasoned that such a cost advantage might overcome the extra shipping costs that a customer in a distant state would have to pay when ordering the company's product.

They reasoned correctly; but how could they solicit this customer's business and service the account once it was established? The cost of a direct man would negate their competitive advantage, so they attempted to have their sales manager or other top executives cover these accounts with occasional visits. This proved to be a very expensive method of operating; it was hard enough to gain a new customer through this arrangement, let alone hold on to him. So these companies turned to reps for help.

When this point was reached in the late forties and early fifties, the chemistry of the companies and the reps started to mix compatibly, slowly at first, and not without many disappointments. Both groups were feeling their way, no real standards existed for terms, contracts, or territories, and there were probably many more unsuccessful associations than there were profitable ones. However, in general, this appears to have been the beginning of truly serious attempts by both companies and reps to develop good working relationships which would be beneficial to all. MANA was formed in 1947, and many of the rep companies listed as members were established in the fifties.

From Opportunity to Necessity

Despite the gradually improving rep programs that companies have developed over the past 20 or 25 years, there's still some uncertainty and confusion in the minds of many business owners and their sales managers as to exactly what the advantages are to adopting a sales rep program. A concise explanation of these advantages was given by Lee Walters,* former president of MANA, who expressed the view that reps can offer five unique services that no one else can provide: (1) A rep can give a manufacturer a predetermined fixed sales cost since sales commissions are based on goods shipped; (2) the rep has his own built-in incentive program: the profit motive; (3) he provides essential local sales management; (4) he gives the manufacturer a trained sales force; and (5) he offers the manufacturer immediate access to a new market.

I'd like to add a sixth service to Lee's list. The rep system gives the manufacturer a *permanently located* sales force. How important is this factor? Ask any sales manager who has spent $30,000 to $50,000 over a two-year period training a bright, energetic, and promising salesman to handle one of the provinces only to have him leave for a better job in another part of the country, or worse yet, accept a position with a similar firm in the same area in which he was selling. He then becomes a potent competitor.

Although it does happen, it's rare for a sales rep to take a "better offer" from a competitor, unless you've really let him down. He wants to succeed with your line; he's spent a lot of his own time and money promoting it to his current customers, and to start all over with a competitor is not an enticing prospect. There's absolutely no incentive for a rep to leave his marketing territory. He started his business there, he has nurtured it there, and he has made it successful there. To pull up stakes and leave for another part of the country is unthinkable; all the contacts he developed over his years in the area would be lost. It has no practical values for him at all. The direct man, on the other hand, has no such financial or emotional ties to a given area, and if someone comes along with grass that may be slightly greener than yours, actual or imagined, you may be out that $30,000 to $50,000 with very little to show for it.

Let's now examine the five advantages that Lee Walters mentioned for proof of their validity.

A rep can give a manufacturer a predetermined fixed sales cost. Our own experience is typical and we'll refer to it often throughout the

* "In The Field," *Agency Sales*, December 1971, pp. 2, 4.

book, although deviations from it will also be recognized. In the lines our agency handles, fabricated metal products, the commission averages around 5 percent. The companies we service can easily work this into their cost estimates with reasonable assurance that their competitors are using about the same figure. If they don't get a particular job, there's no sales cost. If a direct sales force is employed, the sales overhead stays fairly constant and, as sales fall off in slower times, this overhead cost becomes a larger portion of each job. This makes the price less competitive or the operation less profitable.

In times of lesser demand, it's unlikely that sales cost will be reduced substantially because the thing needed most is more sales, and this means a good, capable sales force. Conversely, as times become better, sales costs rise; even more salesmen are needed to exploit the better business conditions. With this comes a little more entertaining of customers and a more relaxed attitude on the part of the sales force when it comes to selling expenses. The steady increase in sales costs is of little concern to the company using commissioned reps. The established commission rate is a known cost based on sales only, and it's comforting to a rep-oriented manufacturer to have one less fluctuating cost to worry about.

The rep has his own built-in incentive program. The incentive, of course, is our commission. To receive commissions we must sell the products of the companies we represent. Every time we get an order we are monetarily rewarded. When the direct man makes a sale he may get brownie points toward a year-end raise plus perhaps some incentive bonus based on a quota or forecast, but this is not the same incentive as we reps have.

In our case our principals don't have to dream up wild schemes or green stamp promotions to get us to sell; the anticipated commissions are sufficient. This is a direct saving in cost and energy for the principal and his sales manager who can concentrate on other problems. As a matter of fact, most reps don't respond well to incentive programs, other than an increase in commission.

The rep provides essential local sales management. You're there and we're here. Sure, you may have some business in a given area and feel quite certain that you can hold on to it through good telephone communications and occasional visits. But without a local sales rep who can stay on top of events as they occur and who may even be selling some of his other lines to your customer, you're taking a chance. And if you start neglecting that customer, you're really vulnerable.

I like nothing better than to discover that my competition at a customer's plant doesn't have a local rep or salesman. This means a real opportunity for me. I may be able to spot some disenchantment with my competitor's product or service long before he does, particularly if he's used to working with one or two people at the company. Being local, I may have contacts throughout the plant who'll give early-warning signs of trouble. In consequence, all other things being equal, my company has a definite edge over the long pull because I'm in closer touch with the day-to-day operations of the customers in my territory.

My principal also has a point of contact in the area for his customers. In emergency situations I'm able to reach expert personnel at the plant or at home because of my complete knowledge of my company's operation. Once, on a critical air delivery of a badly needed component for a customer's disabled machine, I was able to call the assistant sales manager at home on a Saturday morning and get the name of the airline the part had been shipped by. The customer was then able to locate his part the same day at the freight carrier's local depot and have his machine working early Monday morning, eliminating two days of costly down time. This is just one example of the many services a local rep can offer at no extra cost to the principal.

The rep gives the manufacturer a trained sales force. The rep you hire is probably either a former sales manager or a salesman who took the plunge. All the costs involved in teaching him the selling trade were borne by a former employer. Your company is the beneficiary of not only the expense involved in his training but the learning period during which he did not earn the money paid him.

Each rep had to learn all the things you had to learn. Then he had to polish these skills to the point of being capable of supporting himself strictly on the sales he makes. True, there may be some training costs that you'll have to absorb, but these will be related to product knowledge.

In all probability, because a rep tends to associate himself with companies making compatible but not competitive products, your product line will be only a slight variation from one of those he's handling now. In this case, a short briefing on the peculiarities of your line as opposed to the similar line may be all that's initially necessary from a product knowledge view, although thorough knowledge of your company's capabilities, policies, and procedures should follow at an in-plant briefing as promptly as possible.

As far as basic sales training is concerned, you're covered. A good rep, however, is always anxious to learn of specific instances where an alteration of basic sales techniques has been successful in selling your product. Each company has examples of these personalized approaches that should be passed along to the receptive rep.

The rep offers the manufacturer immediate access to a new market. As any sales manager knows, smokestack chasing in a new territory is one of the most discouraging jobs that can be thrust on a man. It can be done, of course, but even a seasoned direct man must receive some real incentives to make him pull up roots and venture into a new untried marketing area that you've decided to penetrate. Turning the same job over to a novice can be sheer suicide and can bring tears to the eyes of the controller as month after month he scans the sales expense sheet from the new territory.

The alternative, and a good one, is to go the rep route. The rep you employ may have worked his territory for up to 20 years. Our 20-year veteran may have spent 15 years as a direct salesman for a company with a product line similar to yours. At the other extreme we may have a one- or two-year man who has taken over a well-established family rep business. In either case, your company is dealing with a man whose agency is familiar with his territory.

A good example of taking the alternative route is provided by one of our firms, a finely managed company selling well in its own five-state area. This firm had some business in Texas and decided it could be competitive on a larger scale. It was ready to come in with both feet.

The company's product line consists of custom manufactured parts that are small, inexpensive, and produced in large quantities. There's usually a long time lag between an initial call and an order, since the customer must pay the company for expensive tooling to make the parts and most customers don't obligate themselves to this extent without a great deal of investigation and value analysis, plus continued care and servicing from the salesman.

A good direct man in Texas might realistically cost our principal $25,000 per year in salary and expenses. Even with good day-to-day direct coverage, a sales volume of $500,000 for this particular product would be difficult to reach by the end of one year, or even three to four years; but this is what it would take, based on a 5 percent sales cost or commission, to support that man in the field.

Taking this down the road a bit, let's say that at the end of four years our direct man has reached his goal of $500,000 in sales and is now self-supporting. Over this four-year period the company has invested $100,000 in that man, which is a sizable risk and an almost impossible investment for most small firms. In addition, since this is what we term a job-shop firm where profit margins are small, it's questionable whether or not this investment would ever be returned.

A commissioned rep, of course, would not be devoting all his time to this one firm; but overshadowing this discrepancy in concentration on the principal's line is the rep's ability to penetrate the market much faster because of the customer relationships he had developed during his years in the market. He may or may not build up to the same volume in the same time as a direct man would, but the company will certainly have avoided a very large investment in a direct man who by no means could guarantee successful market penetration. But the real cause for concern is the stability of the direct man. His departure from the job, for any reason, could diminish the company's sales continuity and endanger its substantial investment.

My friend, the president of this firm, never fails to rib me good-naturedly by saying he's not sure "this is the way to go." And just as often I tell him he has no choice; this is the only way to go if he wants to get into the Texas market without throwing the dice, which are already loaded against him.

Making It in the Real World

To me, the most interesting aspect of any rep firm is how it got its start. Most firms start as one-man operations, but as the individual becomes more successful he becomes busier and ultimately needs help. Here he either enlists a partner or hires a man outright, probably on a commission and draw arrangement. (A RepSurvey I took as part of gathering information for this book shows that the average rep agency consists of 2.2 salesmen but only 1.3 owners or partners.)

One of the earliest reps, James Buchanan Brady, more familiarly known as "Diamond Jim," had a very propitious entry into the ranks. In his book about Brady,* Parker Morrell relates that in 1885 Brady was a successful salesman for Manning-Maxwell-Moore when Simpson Fox, owner of Leeds Forge Co. of England, came to this country to sell his new truck for use under railroad cars. He had absolutely no success and was about to give up when his friend Charles Moore, head of Manning-Maxwell-Moore, referred him to Brady. Brady and Fox dined that very evening and on Fox's departure for England the next day Brady held a contract awarding him 33⅓ percent commission on all Fox trucks sold in the United States or Canada. With such an extraordinary incentive, Brady was on his way to his first million.

Not many present-day reps have such auspicious beginnings nor, with today's tax rates, the chance to become millionaires; but even among "typical" reps, it seems that no two got started in the same manner. Very few sold the old homestead, took their life savings, and went into the rep business.

Harry Renick of Houston, a former sales engineer for a forging company, felt the urge to go out on his own but didn't have sufficient funds to start his agency. However, he knew people at a midwest metal-fabricating company that needed a rep in the Southwest, and he worked out a retainer with them to cover his salary and expenses until commissions exceeded the retainer. With his knowledge of the metalworking business, Harry soon reached this goal and today has a fine business with headquarters in Houston.

Harold McCrone of Annapolis is a "two-timer." That's not as bad as it sounds. Harold entered the rep business twice and made a go of it both times. To be truthful, once he had started his own agency he never really left it; but for a while he became so involved in a secondary business that his first love, a manufacturers' rep career, took a back seat to his managerial obligations.

Originally, having been limited to a maximum income by the company he worked for, Harold took his total cash assets of $350 and left with his family for a two-week vacation to think things out. Wanting to capitalize on his technical abilities in the industrial equipment field, he decided his best bet would be to become a sales rep. Supporting himself with the remainder of the commissions due him from his em-

* *Diamond Jim* (New York: Simon and Schuster, 1934), pp. 46–47.

ployer, he sought out allied lines to represent. Soon he was self-supporting and on his way to an income limited only by his own initiative.

Not satisfied to leave well enough alone, he spotted product needs that were not being filled by current manufacturers and set about fabricating his own products to fill these needs. This resulted in his becoming a manufacturer and a stocking distributor as well as a rep. Eventually, with 48 employees to care for and look after, Harold felt he was getting far away from his original goal and in 1969 sold his manufacturing business to several of his employees and entered the rep field for a "second time." Today, having realized a comfortable income from the sale of his business, he's able to represent quality firms of his choosing and concentrate on doing a good job for firms whose products he enjoys selling.

Dave McBride of Dallas, who is all of 26 years old, is proof that you don't have to be a sales manager for 20 years before being able to make it as a rep. Dave had youth, timing, and product knowledge all working for him at the same time. While servicing Southwestern dairies for a prominent packaging firm and another organization selling dairy ingredients, he learned that a major company was seeking to change its marketing concept. A phone call to the owner, who he knew from previous associations, put him in business overnight. Two more established and related lines followed along a short time later.

Establishing a clientele of 100 dairies in five states takes a lot of time and hard work, but at 26 Dave relishes the opportunity to carve out a rep career at an age when many young men are just beginning to enter the job market.

Regardless of how they began their agencies, all these men and their peers had one thing in common: a fierce desire to establish their own business. However varied the forces driving them to act on their own and become independent of the corporate family—at least to some degree—the end results were the same: a business of their own. It stands to reason that a man so intent on an independent career that he'd seek almost any means to fulfill this desire can be a potent ally for an organization that can effectively aid him to reach his goal. That is why the manufacturers' representative style of selling in today's business community is so imaginative and powerful.

Because of the rep's individuality, however, you'll find that the mere act of hiring him is a radical departure from the routine hiring of a company salesman. And motivating him to bring you the results you expect requires a whole new set of rules. But if you're willing to adjust your techniques to those indigenous to the rep profession, a great future lies ahead for you and your company.

2

WHAT IS A SALES REP?

A portrait of the successful self-employed salesman

Before studying the methods of hiring and motivating sales reps, you'll need a thorough understanding of the characteristics that make this group of men successful in a highly competitive field. You'll find that working with these independent businessmen can be one of the most puzzling yet challenging jobs you'll ever experience.

A direct salesman—a salaried employee of your firm—is somewhat predictable and relatively easy to hire, train, and supervise. In contrast, a rep is hard to hire, difficult to train, and almost impossible to supervise. The complexities of a rep's personality appear as a constant enigma to the sales manager, but these very complexities are behind the rep's choice of a career and his success at his job. In reviewing the characteristics of this man, you'll begin to appreciate both the subtle and unsubtle differences that separate him from the direct salesman, and you'll learn how to make these differences work to your advantage.

A Rep Is Independent

The primary reason why most reps aren't working as direct salesmen is their intense desire for independence. There may be myriad explanations for this independent streak, ranging from an individual's deep-seated psychological disturbances to his simple wish to spend his time as he sees fit, without interference. Regardless of the reason, sales reps chafe under normal supervision and are often impatient with company policies and restrictions. They have an overwhelming need to direct their own business and personal life; but, in return for this privilege, they'll work harder and longer than the average salesman.

One gentleman in Texas, a rep for some 40 years and now 82 years old, has become wealthy through his success in the business. He could have comfortably retired years ago, yet I still see him in purchasing offices, not just visiting and reminiscing, but actively selling and selling well. Frankly, he still outsells me. When this man reached 65, one of his major principals attempted to put him out to pasture. It terminated his contract and tried to handle its customers directly from the home office. In no time at all this spry rascal was handling a competitive line, and he gradually reduced his former principal to an ineffective force in the Texas market. His independence of action, impossible for a direct man, brought him renewed income and continuing enjoyment in his selling career.

A 1964 study * prepared by Michigan State University Graduate School of Business Administration showed that the average owner of a small manufacturing business had great difficulty with interpersonal relationships and authority figures. Many of these men started their own business because of their inability to work within the framework of the corporate organization. Some of them began with partners, but sooner or later the partnerships were dissolved, reinforcing the researchers' theory that it was absolutely necessary to their emotional well-being that they be in complete control of what they were doing.

There is, I believe, a resemblance between the owners of small businesses included in this study and manufacturers' representatives. I know many reps who could not exist for long within the corporate environment. The independence of action offered by the operation of their own sales agency, however, does seem to provide sufficient fulfillment for this need.

Many reps work well with a partner or two. They don't appear to have the deep-seated craving for complete control that the owners of

---

* Orvis F. Collins and David G. Moore, with Darab B. Unwalla, *The Enterprising Man* (Lansing, Mich.: Michigan State University, 1964).

small businesses revealed in the study. This modified independence is a definite advantage to the sales manager and his company. The rep is free to use his own individual method of selling, which is often more productive than a direct man's stereotyped approach. He also feels independent enough to make constructive comments on the principal's performance; these should be accepted by that company in the spirit in which they're offered, for the good of all concerned. Further, as a salesman foremost, the rep is accustomed to using the techniques of that profession: persuasion, cooperativeness, and compromise. This talent, coupled with his modified independence, makes him a unique extension of any organization.

A Rep Is Self-Disciplined

As a sales manager you have regular hours at the office. You're expected to arrive in the morning and leave at the end of the day. In other words, you must meet certain standards that are part of your job, and regular violation of these standards can alter your future with the company.

The rep has no one looking at the clock when he arrives at his office, or strolls from his kitchen to the room at home that he uses as an office. No boss speaks to him about an early departure from the office or notices his absence on a particularly good golfing day. He can take two hours for lunch every day if he chooses, or have an affair with his secretary without undue public notice, at least as far as his job is concerned. No one can actually fire him for such actions, but a rep whose business life follows such an irregular pattern is on the road to retirement—forced retirement—for lack of funds.

Excluding a small minority to whom success has perhaps come too fast, reputable reps will put in a full day and spend even more time on the job than direct men. On salary, direct men can in good conscience adhere to a fairly fixed schedule, although the more successful among them are those who put in whatever number of hours are necessary. The rep cannot coast. There's no personnel office or accounting department to help him; he has to get the job done by himself. He's chief cook and bottle washer, and, if he's to spend the maximum selling hours in the field, he must burn some midnight oil to finish his other duties.

However, a smart rep will also take time away from his job for relaxation: all work and no play is a bad combination for anyone. But he'll discipline himself to take these opportunities when they least affect his selling routine—perhaps a few days around the Christmas holiday, or a timely vacation when he knows his major customers are taking inventory.

To survive as an independent agent, a rep must learn early to conserve his working capital. There are no reimbursable expenses in his business; they all come out of his own pocket. His travel, phone, and entertainment costs must be closely controlled and analyzed monthly for excessive waste. Trips must be planned for maximum sales results; no hundred-mile jaunts just to have lunch with a favorite customer unless such an expense can be justified by sales potential. Long-distance phone calls must be measured against their overall benefit to him and his principals.

Entertainment expenses are always tough to control. Reps are people too; they prefer one person's company over another's. It's tempting to take a good friend to lunch often, even though his account is small and has no real potential. Such entertaining must be nipped in the bud—and it usually is when the rep carefully analyzes his monthly entertainment expenses. By the same token the rep cannot be cheap about his expenses. A good rep will always spend more, rather than less, to avoid offending a customer or losing a lucrative relationship, or if there's no business now but plenty down the road. But he's ever watchful against a regular trend toward overspending in this category.

Taken as a group, successful reps have more self-discipline than direct salesmen. This has come about out of necessity, not from an inherent desire to deny attention to any portion of their business. This trait will serve you well; the self-discipline of your reps is a major key to their consistency of operation in the field.

A Rep Is Ambitious

It has often been noted that a usual concomitant to ambition is desire for power. And power means the ability to control people. Apart from the political arena, the most fertile ground for practicing power over people is found in the corporate structure. The executive who takes pleasure in exercising the power of his position is also endowed with an ambitious personality. The corporate executive is well suited to travel up the organization chart; his coupling of ambition with desire for power has helped him in his inexorable drive toward corporate supremacy.

Our rep has ambition too, but unlike the corporate executive he has no desire or need for power. His ambition is directed toward satisfying other needs: for example, for security and independence. And whereas the corporate executive cannot envision leaving his position of power for a rep's life, even though it could potentially mean more money and independence, our rep would be very reluctant to accept a salaried executive position.

There's no need to make a case for ambition; it's always a desired trait in a salesman. But it's important to understand that the rep's ambition poses no danger to interpersonal relationships between him and the personnel of your company. He has no interest in the internal politics of your organization unless they adversely affect his ability to earn commissions from the sale of your products.

A Rep Is Proud

Man, is he proud! But then what person who thoroughly enjoys his work isn't proud of it? I've yet to discover a rep who's not perfectly happy in his unique profession. Question a rep about his work and he'll lean back with a smile of satisfaction and tell you it's a great job, full of rewards. He'll admit he works hard but then point out how his dedication has paid off. He'll regale you with tales of his sales prowess and big deals, then expound on the basic philosophies all reps should pursue to be successful (these philosophies of course vary greatly from one rep to another).

But he'll gloss over the long nights away from home, the buyers that don't buy from him, the principals with whom he has parted company, and the fact that luck may have played a large part in his original success. I say original success because I can cite case after case where some break, or some freak of timing, propelled a man into the rep business. He may never have entered it without this one happenstance. His continuing success, however, is by and large of his own making and he knows it, and he'll tell you so.

Another powerful stimulus to the rep's pride is his wife. Chances are excellent that she's had more than a little to do with his success. In the beginning she probably helped with the paperwork, bookkeeping, and phone answering, and she certainly provided the encouragement and resolve needed to face the many disappointments that are a part of getting started. Many wives continue to help out even when financial necessity no longer exists.

I recall one evening in my sales manager days, having dinner with one of my reps in his home. About the time coffee was served I realized we had discussed business throughout the entire meal, and I apologized to his wife for being so inconsiderate. She replied, with obvious sincerity, that she found our discussion very interesting. Only then did it dawn on me that she had been an active participant in our exchange of ideas. Her comments and observations came so naturally and were so pertinent that I hadn't been aware of the full extent of her participation. It was clear that this perceptive lady was very close to her husband's business life. I find this not at all unusual in sales reps' families. If a sales manager or owner phones his rep at home in the evening and his wife answers, she'll know who the caller is, he can count on it.

When my partner and I started our rep business, we purchased a franchised carpet-cleaning business that would pay for the groceries while we scouted up companies to represent. Although we had a nice, modest, money-losing company of 15 employees, we never seemed particularly enthusiastic about telling people we were carpet cleaners. The business was foreign to us and we weren't really happy in our work.

When our rep business became self-sustaining and we were able to sell our carpet-cleaning enterprise back to the franchising company (which was making all the money anyhow), we breathed a sigh of relief. At last again in a business with which we were familiar, we could labor with confidence and assurance in our capabilities and, in this case, pride in our work. Habits are hard to break, however, and even today, when taking our customers to one of the finer restaurants, we still tend to glance at the condition of the carpet before looking at the menu.

The rep's pride in his profession means that he's in his chosen line of work and he'll remain there as long as good business and good health allow him to. And to you this means a permanently located sales rep.

A Rep Is Selective

Here we're talking primarily about the rep's selection of the type of firms he wants to represent. Early in the game his ability to be selective will leave something to be desired. When starting his agency he'll probably concentrate on quantity rather than quality. A beginning rep needs lines badly, and almost any manufacturer with a line slightly allied to the rep's overall agency sales concept will be welcomed, perhaps mistakenly. Since there are more lines available than there are good reps to handle them, our beginner may soon find himself trying to sell a variety of products that may or may not be of good quality and may be unsuited to his marketing area and sales capabilities.

If he's fortunate enough to survive in business for a year or two, his selective processes will become much more sophisticated because of his experiences. His decisions will then begin to benefit not only his agency but his new principals as well. He's better qualified, although never perfectly qualified, to analyze a prospective principal, the principal's product line, and his own customers' needs, and he can make a reasoned, intelligent decision to accept or decline a line.

Occasionally even a seasoned pro will make a mistake or, pressured by a company that has heard good things about him, will accept a line although his deep gut reaction tells him not to. Usually this ends up with both parties sorrier but wiser. However, on the positive side, it does contribute a learning experience that can be drawn on if a similar situation arises in the future. A rep's ability to be selective with both customers and principals may also be a valuable asset for your own company because, properly used, it can mean time and money to you.

Recently I followed up a quote one of our companies made to a local firm. "You're twelfth high on our list of 15 bidders," the buyer informed me. On hearing this I suggested that we be removed from his inquiry list, giving as a reason that on the basis of our high quote we would not be a competitive source for him. The real reason, of course, was that I didn't think my principals wanted to devote costly estimating time to firms going out on 15 bids for their requirements. As one of my sales managers said recently when we were discussing this very situation, "Among 15 bids, someone is going to make a mistake, and he'll no doubt wind up with the work and a loss on the job."

In cases like this, judicious selectivity by the rep allows the principal to avoid wasting valuable resources on a buyer who's unskilled in his profession and who, at this stage of his career, would not bring the principal profitable business. Of course, in a few months I'll check back with his firm to see if the buyer is still around and to assess the firm's potential as a customer in light of any changes that may have occurred. Perhaps the buyer will be gone or will have experienced a change of heart, brought about by other responsible salesmen, that will justify a renewed solicitation of his business.

A Rep May Be a Maverick

Among my acquaintances are several gentlemen in our business who could never snag a job as direct salesmen. Appearance and manners alone would probably rule them out. One is a gum chewer who talks incessantly while snapping his gum and takes all day to get to the point, punctuating every other sentence with a nervous laugh. Another is an extreme egotist; my staying time with him is a short lunch or a predinner cocktail. The third salesman berates management people at sales meetings, exposing their imagined deficiencies for all to see and offering cynical suggestions on how they can improve their performances. When the meetings break up, his colleagues avoid him because of his overbearing personality.

But all three men are still tolerated by their principals, even though the sales managers maintain as little contact with them as possible. Why? Because all three consistently bring in good, profitable sales for their companies. The first rascal may drive you up the wall with his nervous habits, but if you're a customer with a problem in his specialty field, he can spot it immediately and show you how to solve that problem and perhaps save some money doing it, of course using his firm's products to accomplish the job.

The second man, through years of patient, diligent effort, has cultivated people in high places in the one industry he serves, and when the chips are down on a big order he usually brings it in. The third rep has only one virtue: insistence on good, prompt service for his customers. He'll get the principal's president out of bed at midnight, if that's what it takes to make a critical delivery as scheduled.

In all three cases we have men who couldn't fill out a psychological test, let alone pass one. Their crudities, inconsiderateness, and all-round boorishness wouldn't qualify them for a preliminary sales interview. But despite all these handicaps, they've somehow managed to concentrate their energies on one outstanding trait that has enabled them not only to make a living but to prosper.

These men are outstanding exceptions to the average rep whose personality is more closely aligned to industry's image of the professional salesman. The rep is usually courteous, considerate, and a pleasurable companion. But the point about the maverick is that he could be your top sales producer. The above-mentioned gum chewer is the No. 1 rep for his major principal; he annually sells over a million dollars of a very competitive product. While I don't recommend hiring reps with such distinct personality disorders, in certain markets and circumstances it could pay off. You'll have to be the judge of whether or not it's worth it.

A Rep Is Security Conscious

A popular misconception in industry is that the security-minded businessman stays tied to the corporation's apron strings for fear of losing his fringe benefits and overall security, whereas the high-risk individual goes into business for himself. Not so. A good friend, a scriptwriter specializing in industrial films, had just left his firm for a crack at freelancing. I asked him about the break from steady employment. "No damn supervisor is going to control my future; I want to be able to determine my own financial well-being," he replied. That ended an argument over who was security-minded and who was not.

During our association over a script for a film my company was making, my friend would often refer to the closeness of his "point of destitution." His preoccupation with the subject even prompted him to bring it up at a dinner party one evening. He went around the table asking each couple to project how long they could exist at their present level if the money stopped coming in. He seemed pleased by the shocked reaction of his dinner companions when they realized they were not as secure as they had imagined.

Many of the reps I know have this same preoccupation. They're not necessarily as honest or self-examining about it as my friend, but they do want to be the determining force in their own financial future and don't want an employer to have control over what they view as an important factor in their life.

In a rep's mind, the high-risk man is the corporate employee who can be summarily fired and stripped of his income and accompanying benefits overnight. Because of his chosen profession, the rep believes he has insurance against any such eventuality. He may lose one line or principal, but his strength lies in numbers; he constantly endeavors to spread his risk so that no one principal can put him out of business by terminating his contract.

However, Mike Lumpkin, a prominent Dallas CPA familiar with reps' financial secrets, points out that, despite their efforts and desires, most reps are dependent on one or two lines for a major share of their income; thus the extent of their security is seldom as complete as they'd like it to be. And I'm certain that a person who's so security conscious will never be completely free from financial concern, regardless of the amount of business he generates or the number of lines he handles. But driven remorselessly by this compulsive desire to reach the unattainable goal of ultimate financial security, your rep will continually push to make more sales and do a better job for you and your customers.

A Rep Is Secretive

Sorry, but it's true. Your inquiries into the nature of a rep's other lines, his relationships with his customers, and his daily routine will bring little information. In his defense, there's substantial justification for his attitude. At one time or another almost every rep has been burned after divulging too much about his activities.

The rep stands alone and usually works alone. He often feels like a besieged combatant who not only is fighting his competitors but must keep an eye on his rear flank as well. Knowing that some companies change reps as often as they change sales managers, he makes wariness a daily habit and attempts to keep his own counsel. Only rarely will he give his principals any information beyond what relates directly to the business at hand.

Because of a large order that's hanging fire or a complicated problem, a rep may be required to devote an entire week to one customer and one principal. Awareness of this concentrated attention on products other than theirs can unduly upset the rep's other principals and cause them to think he's neglecting their company's interests. They must realize, however, that in similar circumstances a good rep will devote an equal amount of time to their interests.

The rep's customers are his life-sustaining contacts. Any effort on your part to discover some of the closely guarded techniques he uses with certain customers will be an exercise in futility. As a sales manager I've listened to more intelligent-sounding double-talk from reps than most businessmen can imagine. However, the rep will be as helpful as possible in answering any general questions you may ask about a customer or a prospect, because teamwork is the essence of success in business; but forgive him for being purposely vague about some aspects of his operation.

The epitome of secretiveness may be observed in a conversation between two reps working the same area for different principals. An unwritten rule seems to prohibit the exchange of information in such a discussion beyond the normal courtesies and the weather.

You really shouldn't be surprised by a rep's reluctance to discuss most of his activities with you. Consider him as a business entity similar to your own. Your company keeps its customer list in sacred trust and would be hesitant to discuss it freely. Nor does it divulge sales policies or competitive advantages to its competitors. Similarly, your rep jealously protects his right to privacy regarding many of the operations of his agency. What you don't know can't hurt him!

A Rep Is Entrepreneurial

Entrepreneurial is hardly a word that rolls off the tongue, but it describes the coming together of all the individual qualities necessary for running a successful rep operation. While each of the characteristics previously discussed is important in itself, the entrepreneurial personality is created by an imaginative blending of them all, plus a few more.

A direct salesman can do a good job without the benefit of this elusive entrepreneurial quality. He need not concern himself with the day-to-day operations of his company. He can go into the field knowing that the production, accounting, and other departmental operations of his firm are in the hands of specialists.

On the other hand, in addition to his selling chores, the rep is responsible for all aspects of his sales agency including office management, advertising, accounting, public relations, communications, community relations, and tax matters. To deal with these tasks successfully and stay in business through the lean years takes hard-headed ability, a fact not always apparent to the ambitious novice who looks longingly at the rep profession. To him it appears that several good lines and a smiling face will insure success. He tends to minimize or overlook the contribution of management know-how to the security and growth of a rep business.

Many tales are told of top-notch salesmen making the jump to their own business and enjoying much early success, only to find that salesmanship alone is ultimately not enough. Take the man who started off with three good capital equipment lines, thanks to his good performance as a direct salesman. These product lines could be sold only to large oil companies and required contact with each purchasing agent several times a year. This was fairly simple, since the salesman had built up a good reputation over the years and orders came often and big. He was soon worth many hundreds of thousands of dollars and had a brilliant future, and he wondered why he hadn't taken the plunge years before.

However, instead of concentrating on good agency management aimed toward consolidation of his gains and steady growth, he relaxed. He overestimated his own talents and underestimated the amount of work necessary to maintain his success. With relaxation came too many days at the club and at the bar. Gradually it became obvious to his principals that the rep was living handsomely off his large commissions but was no longer selling to and servicing their customers in the fashion required for continued business. In addition, his days and nights at the bar began to take their toll and he went rapidly downhill, losing his principals one after another. Our friend was a good salesman, but he lacked one ingredient essential to successful entrepreneurship: self-discipline. His inability to control his own actions ultimately led to the loss of his business.

This case is an extreme example, of course, but equally foolish actions are performed by capable men who should know better. Some reps concentrate too much on one customer, or one purchasing man, or one principal. They don't have the foresight to develop a well-balanced agency based on a moderation of dependencies. Thus, if their customer goes out of business or their purchasing friend is removed from his position or their principal desires to hire someone else, they experience an immediate and drastic drop in income. A Dallas rep did almost all his business with a close personal friend in purchasing at one of the larger aerospace firms; the purchasing man lost his job and the rep lost his entire business, almost overnight.

Mistakes of this nature are foreign to the true entrepreneur. Like the company that attempts to avoid the peaks and valleys characteristic of any one industry by diversifying its product line and its customers, the intelligent rep seeks to even out his dependence on any one area of his business. In searching for effective reps to serve you, seek out this type of individual. His stability, a result of his all-round capabilities, can lead to a long and successful association.

A Rep Is Un-Average

You should be prepared and willing to accept an occasional departure from the norm when dealing with your reps. They may be outspoken, sometimes to the point of rudeness; but frequently their frank appraisals of weaknesses in your company's policies prove to be extremely valuable. These same appraisals may not be readily made by salaried employees, who fear they'll incur the displeasure of their superiors, damage their careers, or even lose their jobs.

Just prior to composing this chapter I wrote an honest letter to one of our principals about our lack of results over the past nine months. I outlined the broken promises and the tardy quotations given to me over this period and explained how these affect our relationships with our good customers. Naturally I'm reluctant to solicit any more business for this firm from buyers who have come to rely on my word and the performance of my other principals. Ironically, the company in question is prominent in its field, but perhaps it regards the Texas market as not of sufficient importance to warrant the service it offers in other areas. In the two years of our association with this firm, the sales manager has not once visited our territory.

Could an employed field salesman take as hard a line as this with his boss? Not likely. However, since this company represents only a portion of our commissions, we can assume the risk of being fired—or terminated as it's known in our business—in return for the possibility of increased assistance and larger commissions. This probably comes under the heading of independence: we can take such chances because of our relatively independent position.

The characteristics outlined in this chapter must be viewed as those of an average rep. But, as you know, averages are often determined from extremes, and the average model that emerges from the extremes is completely "un-average." You must therefore be ready to accept behavior at both ends of the spectrum.

For example, a particular rep may be so self-disciplined that he works literally night and day on your behalf, but he may also show an abnormal amount of independence, even to the point of causing problems within your organization. This poses a dilemma. Should you hang on to him because of his effectiveness in the marketplace, or should you forgo that benefit because it may not compensate for the internal problems his independence creates? By watching for the extremes of personality when hiring, you can prevent the necessity for agonizing decisions later on. You're therefore going to have to exercise more perception and discretion in hiring a rep than you would when employing a direct man.

By accustoming yourself in advance to the variations in character and personality that are typical of our breed, you can select men with qualities closest to the norm. By using extra care in this selection, you'll be taking a positive step toward creating a uniform and productive rep organization. Your relations and communications will be smoother and more trouble-free with a group of reps having similar characteristics than with a group whose dissimilar personalities will require individual attention and consideration.

3

A PRERECRUITMENT
SELF-ANALYSIS

Can your company pass the test?

Now that you've found out what makes a rep function, you're already
half way home. If you still think your psyche is capable of withstand-
ing the complexities involved in developing a rep sales program, you
must next take a critical look at your own organization. As the man in
charge of the program, you may be fully qualified for this challenge,
but whether or not your company and its personnel are ready or qualified for this venture into a new marketing style is more important than
your own positive attitude. All the good intentions in the world can't
overcome handicaps that may already be built into your organization
and that may be difficult or impossible to overcome.

Facing this question honestly can prevent the needless expense of a
program that will eventually fail. It can also result in a decision to
proceed that will mean substantial growth, increased profits, and expanding opportunities that appeared unattainable prior to your investigation of the possibilities of a successful rep sales program.

To help you with this decision, and to help those firms whose rep
program is not working out as well as they had hoped it would, I've
established a set of questions that can provide important clues to the
ultimate wisdom of developing, or staying with, a rep sales program.
In pondering these questions and some of the reasons for my asking
them, you'll find that your answers will indicate rather quickly

whether or not you and your company possess the characteristics needed to insure a reasonably successful program.

You need not be perfect on all counts. If your company appears to qualify in the main, some of the minor faults, which you'll recognize as you go along, can be gradually overcome. The important ability, of course, is to recognize those faults and to take steps to correct them.

Are You Merely Looking for a New World to Conquer?

Occasionally a sales manager will look longingly toward one industrial area where his product should be in high demand because of a concentration of a certain type of industry in that geographical location. For instance, a new textile machinery firm may be interested in the Southwest, where there are numerous makers of clothing and related items. The sales manager, unable to afford a direct man and his expenses, concludes that hiring an experienced rep will serve to introduce him to the market at a fraction of the cost of a direct salesman. His intention may be to switch to a direct man when the rep's commissions reach the level at which the direct man can be supported.

Aside from being unfair to the rep and bordering on the unethical, such a policy may also prove to be foolish. Suppose that the rep develops a good volume for this company and is then replaced by a salaried salesman. Several things can happen.

The new salesman may fall on his face and lose vital business to the competition, perhaps even to the rep who was replaced and who took on a competitive line. Afraid that a second salaried salesman might prove equally disastrous, the sales manager may decide to revert to a rep in that area. This is easier said than done, as word travels fast in these circles—while the sales manager may pick up a new, untried rep for his line, the professionals will not handle his products. His company's share of the business in that area may fall below the level attained by his original rep.

The sales manager may want to enter another marketing territory and may sincerely wish to go with a good rep and stay with him. But even though they work hundreds of miles apart, reps are becoming better acquainted with each other through seminars and meetings. This means that, despite his good intentions, the sales manager's reputation may have preceded him into an area, and he may be unable to find a good rep willing to take a chance on him. Worse yet, although management changes may bring about an entirely new attitude toward reps, the melody lingers on, and it may take the company a long time to reestablish a credible reputation within the rep field.

How Firm Is Top Management's Commitment?

Unless you own the company, you may embark on the rep route without the full backing of your top management. The president or chairman may have a casual attitude: "Reps might be worth a try; after all, it would be nice to make a few sales out West." Unaware of the long, difficult, and sometimes expensive route we're talking about, your boss may become discouraged after one or two early setbacks and scuttle the whole project.

This leaves you with no sales program and some unhappy reps in the field. The best favor you could do both yourself and the man in charge would be to present him with a copy of this book and insist that he read it from cover to cover before approving your plan for using reps in the sale of your firm's wares.

It would also be wise to scan the AMA course schedule for their periodic seminars on different methods of marketing; these sessions occasionally include a comprehensive review of how to market effectively through manufacturers' representatives. Here you and your peers—some of whom are very successful in this realm—will discuss the pros and cons of using reps.

If, after such a study, your superiors give the green light to your program, they'll be much more tolerant of the occasional setbacks and disappointments that are a part of the implementation of such an ambitious undertaking.

Are You Seriously Interested in the National Market?

A rep of my acquaintance in Texas was asked by a prominent Midwest metal-stamping company to serve as its representative in his territory. His investigation of the firm's capabilities impressed him, and both parties agreed to contract terms.

The rep made a conscientious effort to dig up stamping business for this company and soon obtained inquiries from several of his better customers. However, from the start he noticed a considerable delay between the date of inquiry and the date of quote, sometimes as long as six to eight weeks. By that time, some of the business had already been placed with a competing firm. The rep also had been promised samples on several occasions, and if he received them at all they'd arrive only after several follow-up phone calls.

Another disturbing feature was that the company's quotes always seemed to be high compared with the competition's, although the company was quite successful in its own area, receiving about 10 percent of the business it quoted on, a good figure for that industry.

After a few more months of unsuccessful selling efforts, the truth came out. The rep received copies of seven or eight quotations intended for the company's Chicago rep and mailed to him in error. The quotations had been made within seven to ten days of the inquiry date, a startling contrast to the service received by the Texas rep. The fortuitously acquired documents clearly indicated that the company had no intention of seriously pursuing business in Texas, 1,000 miles from the plant.

As many other firms had done before it, this company used the free services of reps in far-off territories with perhaps two aims: (1) The company wanted a national image, thus increasing its prestige with peer companies and customers in its regional (and effective) marketing area; (2) it hoped to pick up some business in these outer areas if it could make an above-average profit on the sales. With absolutely no intention of making any effort to compete in markets outside its own regional area, this company had still enlisted unsuspecting reps in a charade designed to further its selfish aims.

If your company believes the regional market is where it shines, it should concentrate on hiring reps for that specific area. Taking on reps in other areas with no intention of giving them the same support the company provides to regional reps serves no good immediate purpose and will damage the company's reputation in the long run.

Are You Financially Ready for Expansion?

Properly implementing a sales rep program means gradually increasing the number and value of new orders. Financial planning for this growth is relatively easy if done early and faced realistically. Some small businesses, however, tend to undercapitalize, so that the funds needed to finance this expansion are neither planned for sufficiently in advance nor available when needed. The resultant heavy strain on working capital affects relations with creditors and—when commission payment is delayed—even reps. A careful analysis of your reserve ability by your financial officer or CPA firm is therefore vital to your plans for the increased business to be realized as your new reps begin to develop new customers.

There's always a chance that one of your new reps will hit the jackpot within a few weeks and send in a large order that will tax your financial and production abilities. The temptation to extend yourself to meet this sudden surge of business is too enticing to resist. You should be prepared with a quick source of cash and a frank appraisal of your ability to fill this type of order.

If you don't prepare for such an eventuality, several things could happen, all of them bad. (1) Waiting to pay for your raw materials until you're paid by your customers may mean that your suppliers will tighten their credit reins. (2) Delayed payment of commissions might endanger relations with reps. (3) Inability to quickly increase production might mean missed deliveries, not only to your new customer but to your old customers as well, creating ill will. (4) Large orders go hand in hand with competitive pricing and your costs have to be carefully controlled. Frequently this is difficult because the unusual temporary demand on your plant and personnel can cause overtime, sloppy work, and other cost-increasing inefficiencies.

These kinds of difficulties can be avoided, however, if you'll realistically project your growth, always allowing for the unexpected and initiating in advance the proper financial and production planning.

Can You Control the Growth of Your Rep Program?

Having made the decision to expand their production through a rep program, too many companies try to blanket the country completely and immediately. This so dilutes administrative effort and effectiveness that the program limps along aimlessly; an exhausted sales manager trying to cover all bases soon begins to lose credibility among reps and his own people. No one person or department can go from administering a local sales program to handling a national effort overnight without breakdowns in the process.

Each rep who is signed up needs a surprising amount of attention, particularly if he's good. He wants to know more about the product line, he's interested in any potential prospect lists you may have, and he needs a lot of help to learn your policies and procedures. A sales manager who's out trying to sign up reps all over the country is merely compounding his problem. He's too busy to take care of the reps already in the fold, and his hurrying the selection of future reps works to everyone's disadvantage.

Prior to enlisting reps for his firm, the perceptive sales manager will pinpoint target areas, initially perhaps no more than two or three where he believes his company can compete successfully. He'll then use the various methods outlined in this book to attract the best reps he can find in those territories. Not until he has these men comfortably settled in place should he consider hiring additional reps.

Can Top Management Accept the Rep's Independence?

For strong-willed leaders this can be a crucial question. Having fought a hard battle to bring their company to a leadership position in their industry, some successful entrepreneurs may tend to balk at anything that appears like a loss of control. While employing reps may seem to be a good expansion move, conflicts could arise that would put the program in jeopardy. Attempting to maintain control by one ruse or another, consciously or subconsciously, the chief executive could alienate his rep force.

While most reps will try to give equal selling time to all their principals, this is not always practical; as explained in the preceding chapter, a rep may spend as much as a week on one principal's problem. To a chief executive not accustomed to sporadic allegiance, this type of on-again off-again selling, if discovered, can lead to a highly charged confrontation.

During a recession that hit his company particularly hard, one top man had his regional manager calling us nightly at home for a report on our day's activities in his behalf. Knowing the company was hurting for business while some of our other principals were fully booked, we had made a concentrated selling effort for it, as we would have done for any of our companies in the same circumstances. However, the nightly "report to headquarters" finally became too demanding, and a continuing campaign for one company would not have been fair to our other principals, so we asked to be relieved of our obligations. During that stressful period I personally know of four other reps who left the company because its embrace had become too possessive.

In contrast, other firms have become successful because of the chief executive's ability to delegate. This is our type of man, and with any luck at all he'll have a good, effective rep sales force. Naturally, he's interested in results, but not at any cost. We usually find his sales manager to be cut from the same cloth as his boss, with a steady hand on the tiller, but with the flexibility and ease of administration that makes a rep want to perform for him. Commissions are incentives for us, but working for human, responsive people brings out the best in us: a desire to do our utmost for them in our territory.

If a martinet form of management predominates in a company, good rapport with its reps is unlikely. A sales manager's attempt to administer a rep sales program will be caught in the crossfire between two forces. On one hand his top management will insist on reports, statistics, and other forms of control over the field group. Opposing this will be the reps, who are notoriously neglectful in feeding back trivia. With such a prominent handicap staring the sales manager in the face, he'd be better off remaining with a direct sales force that's more adaptive to a control-conscious management. However, if its top people are comfortable with a looser management style when it comes to sales, then a company should seriously consider taking the rep route.

Can You Tolerate Your Rep's Prosperity?

You probably can, at least in the early stages. It's later on, when the commissions add up, that concerns us.

When commissions are small, companies are happy to pay them. No car expense, no supervision expense, none of the heavy drains on working capital that so often prevent companies from being adventurous: a small price to pay for prospecting a new territory. However, if you've been fortunate in hiring good professional reps, inevitably the sales curve on the chart will start to rise and commissions will begin going up.

At first everyone is happy about this rise—you, top management, and the rep. You, because it shows results, your program is beginning to succeed; top management, because the profit-and-loss statement is improving, and, so far, sales costs have not been too high; the rep, because his expenditure in time and money is beginning to pay off.

One of the comforting thoughts to a rep is that most sales managers understand all the pioneering work that has gone on and are pleased that their reps are now starting to receive a good income. This justifies their original aim, and from here on they have a fixed sales cost. Cost-of-sales projections help in planning further moves, and all in all things look good.

The problems start when other executives and personnel get involved in the schedule of commissions. The president or controller may notice that old Charlie in Detroit was paid $50,000 last year on sales of $1 million. As long as Charlie was in the $10,000 to $20,000 range, no one paid much attention, but now it's obvious that a direct man can be maintained on $35,000 a year, a saving of $15,000. This can start rumblings in the executive suite, and if these are transformed into positive action, they can almost certainly spell the end of a good rep program.

The intention of replacing old Charlie and no other rep, though sincere, is of course shortsighted. Charlie may take the business to a competing firm practically overnight, but the greatest danger lies in the effect the move has on the firm's other reps.

One major fastener firm in my area is making a steady march toward direct men. It camouflages its intentions well, sometimes changing one rep for another, then citing the second rep's ineffectiveness after a short trial period and changing to a direct man. The firm may as well go straight to direct men since its ultimate purpose is obvious to the remaining reps, who are all looking for a new principal to replace it. This clearly can be harmful to the firm, particularly in areas with lower but increasing sales where a direct salesman can't yet be supported.

Numerous examples can be offered for analysis: Hiring a new sales manager to improve sales sends shudders through the rep force; a president who is signing checks for reps that are equal to and are sometimes even larger than his can become mighty unhappy; the operating manager who is told to reduce his operating costs can point a finger at sales commissions as the real culprit. A chapter could be devoted to the dangers in getting too many people involved in rep commissions, in particular those people who don't understand the philosophy of a rep program.

At the very beginning of your rep program make certain that steps are taken to limit the number of personnel directly involved with rep remuneration, or you'll be sorry later on.

Can You Wait for Results?

The rep business is not notorious for overnight successes. As with any other type of selling, even with ready access to a market, your reps will not start flooding your desk with orders.

Simply because your rep has many buying friends in his area doesn't mean they'll press orders on him immediately. The better the buyer the more caution he exhibits. A trusted rep who approaches him with a new supplier lowers his resistance faster than a newcomer to the area would, but the buyer is still responsible for intelligent purchasing decisions, and while he may start sending you inquiries immediately, it may be a few months or even years before he'll take a chance on you. Prior to that he'll have made an investigation of your capabilities.

We know a buyer who we think of as a good friend of ours. We took on a new line consisting of a component our friend's company used in its production line every day. He said he'd like to buy this product from us and set the wheels in motion. First we had to quote a competitive price. Then our company's facilities had to be approved by the engineering department. Since we were in a recession, it was almost a year before the buyer could wangle authorization for an engineer to visit the plant.

I accompanied the engineer to the plant 1,000 miles away, which meant a travel and entertainment expense of over $300. He enthusiastically approved our manufacturing facilities, saying they were far superior to those of the existing suppliers. However, because his firm had received some cancellations of orders for its finished units, our friend had a sufficient supply of the product on hand and on order to feed his production line for six to eight months. Finally, he placed an order for delivery four months later and we received our first commission—about two years after we introduced him to the product. While this is an unusually long time to wait for an order, the incident does point up the great patience and tenacity needed to build a market for your product.

Another example of frustrating delays involves a Texas firm and a rep in the East. In his own territory the rep is enthusiastically welcomed as a knowledgeable and capable technical salesman. His customers rely on his advice, even to the point of changing their component designs at his suggestion to achieve a saving in cost. He agreed to try to sell the Texas firm's product to his customers.

The company received inquiries from the rep's customers almost immediately. Prompt quotes were sent out to over a dozen new potential customers. The first order was received about six months later and the second in eight months. Both were trial orders amounting to less than $500 each in an industry where the average order might be $4,000. It'll probably be another several months before production orders are received.

This happened under the very finest selling conditions possible and illustrates the caution with which knowledgeable buyers proceed in today's competitive selling climate. Generally speaking, when your company invades a new marketing area, even with an established rep, you must be willing to accept a time lag greater than that considered normal in your present marketing areas where your reputation may be well known. Of course, some product lines move faster than others for various reasons: The buyer's investment may be small, the item may be available off the shelf, or it may be so new and exciting that the buyer will take a chance on it almost immediately. If your product is in one of these categories, your wait for orders may be shortened.

Is Your Company Ready for New Challenges?

Selling in new areas and to a greater variety of industries can bring unexpected and sometimes unpleasant experiences. We had just such an experience with the customer mentioned above in the story of our two-year wait for our initial commission. After going through all those trials it would be natural for us to assume we'd live happily ever after, depositing our monthly commissions in the bank and automatically entering new orders month after month. Well, it didn't quite turn out that way.

Our customer had a critical application for his product, a device used in the transportation industry to lessen shock in the handling of merchandise. The device saved many millions of dollars in damage claims against the carriers. Because of the critical function performed by this product, exceptionally stringent quality requirements were spelled out for our company's component. We were personally told by both engineering and purchasing personnel that they meant business and that close inspection would be made of all parts received. We related this emphatically to our principal, well in advance of production, and were assured that no problems would arise.

A few weeks later I was on a business trip and received an urgent message from my office to phone our friend the buyer. With a sinking feeling I made the call and was told that the entire first carload of our product had been rejected. Several months later, after trying and failing to meet the customer's tough quality restrictions at a competitive price, our company declined to accept further orders. This experience meant a loss of about $10,000 a year in commissions to our agency.

It was also an expensive experience for our principal—a fine company, a money-maker that manufactures an excellent product year in and year out. However, even good, experienced firms can make mistakes when trying to penetrate a new market or industry.

A company's failure in its first venture into a new area can be particularly damaging. Competitors are delighted to relate the embarrassing details, shaking their heads in mock concern for "poor old ABC Company having all those troubles over at the wagon-wheel factory." Word does get around, so it's important that you have personnel capable of effectively analyzing the odds and making the right decision when faced with a new challenge.

While our one principal was withdrawing from its unfortunate endeavor, another was working closely with the R&D people at a major oil-tool manufacturer developing a new product destined to save hundreds of thousands of dollars in oil exploration costs. For four years the company's engineering staff worked diligently to perfect the product. Conscious of the long road that lay ahead, the top managers went into the project with their eyes open and confident of the capabilities of their technical personnel. At the end of the fourth year the product was successfully marketed and our customer is placing steadily increasing production orders.

This firm's realistic look at its own ability to see the experimental project through to final completion contrasts strikingly with our other principal's inability to assess its chances of making a known product profitably to extra-stringent quality standards. Reps will welcome your forays into new product ideas and improvements on old ones, but they do ask that you look before you leap so that an intended venture, once undertaken, has a good chance of success.

Can You Adapt to a Rep Program Internally?

One of our best principals uses the services of only one rep firm: ours. Now this is a fine company and its product is of good quality. The response of its staff to questions and problems is immediate. But its internal systems have had great difficulty adapting to us, although there are definite signs that finally, after five years, things may be changing.

Up to now, we'd first hear of a new order from one of our customers when we received a copy of an invoice, when our customer told us, or when the sales manager mentioned it during a phone conversation. We long ago gave up trying to keep records on new orders and shipments from this company. That has hurt us in our dealings with our customers, since we appeared not to be sufficiently aware of what was going on in this company; our lack of information, in turn, was mistaken for a lack of interest. We haven't been more critical of this firm because we know the clerical personnel are really trying, but since they have only one rep they're not rep-oriented.

This is a common occurrence at companies where no prior rep program existed. The foul-ups can occur at all levels, from the secretarial pool to—heaven forbid!—accounts payable. So when you hire your first rep, start an internal training program and ride herd on it for a few months. If copies of orders or other correspondence aren't mailed to the rep, make a commotion and continue to do so until such procedures become routine, which they will.

Can You Provide Technical Assistance in the Field?

Often, on-the-spot technical assistance can clinch an order that has been hanging fire for months. Or a timely visit by a factory man can clear up a long-standing problem that threatens to become a major source of discontent, with a possible loss of business.

Periodic visits to the territory by technical personnel seem to offer no particular problem in theory, but shaking the right man loose, at the right time, is sometimes difficult. While expense is always a factor, we find that small and medium-size companies often place qualified technical personnel in charge of departments, but these men are up to their ears in work. One day in the field means a minimum of a day and a half away from the plant; too many such trips keep the department heads from managing their crews effectively.

Most of the sales managers of our principals come into the territory on fairly regular visits. Fortunately they can handle all but the most technical matters in good fashion. Under such circumstances the availability of technical personnel is less important. However, few reps have the specific knowledge or authority required to handle the technical problems that seem to arise with annoying frequency, so you must be able to provide assistance when it's needed.

Can You Be Patient?

As you've read these questions and tried to answer them in relation to your own company, you should have developed a certain confidence in, or uncertainty about, the feasibility of a rep sales program for your company. If at this point you still have a good many doubts about going ahead, it would be well to wait a few months and observe the workings of your company and its personnel.

Can changes be made here and there that would make your company a more likely candidate for a rep sales program? Perhaps talking over the prospective problems with your top management can effect some changes that would make the program more practical. Discussions with other sales managers or owners of similar but noncompeting companies can be illuminating. You may discover some of the early difficulties they experienced, difficulties you can avoid with prior knowledge of their possibility.

If analysis of the results of your investigation convinces you that most signs are in your favor and your company can fully support this expanded selling effort, then you're ready to begin to try to attract the best reps active in the marketing areas you've pinpointed. You may begin your quest in several ways, but the most productive, for an overall program, is through the medium of advertising.

4

HELP WANTED—
SALES REP

How to reach the top candidates

Advertising will prove to be your best single avenue to making contacts with capable professional reps, and the more wisely you spend the better your odds of finding and hiring a pro. In advertising, spending wisely does not connote cutting corners. Take this ad for example:

> Mfrs. Reps—Southeast mfg. co. prec. mach. pts. stl. brs. for prom. cus. needs dyn. rep org. write Box 234

Mercifully modified to protect the guilty, this ad actually appeared in the classified section of a well-known business publication. It was inserted in abbreviated fashion for one reason—to save money. It ran for several issues, each undoubtedly as unproductive as the preceding ones. The total sum spent, if concentrated on one good ad, would have overwhelmingly outpulled the three or four insertions of the condensed ad.

Since the average rep's income is approximately $43,000, he can be considered in the executive income bracket. This ad would not have attracted an executive of your company, and it's no more likely to attract a good rep. Frankly, neither would most of the advertisements placed by companies seeking qualified reps.

Robert E. Sibson, a management consultant, put an $18,300 price tag on the cost of hiring a middle manager (salary, about $30,000).* Yet many companies go about the task of hiring reps as though they were looking for a trainee for the shipping department. Because of this low-budget approach, these companies will never attract the caliber of rep they'd like.

Once you've committed yourself to assembling a top-notch group of reps, or to complementing your present force, you should budget a reasonable amount of money for advertising. Without such a commitment you'll have great difficulty consistently contacting good rep firms. When you consider how much a good rep can improve your profits—far beyond the modest cost of a good advertising campaign— it doesn't make sense to skimp on this expense.

The Right Place for the Right Ad

Media selection will have a direct bearing on the cost of your campaign, so before earmarking the necessary funds it's wise to choose the publications you'll be using. After sending for advertising rate sheets and deciding on the ad size and number of insertions, you can accurately figure your costs.

Several different publications may be used effectively to attract good reps. The two that offer the most exposure to professional reps are *The Wall Street Journal* and *Agency Sales* magazine. Also of importance are trade journals and local newspapers in the territory you're targeting. Each of these should be considered on its own merits. The information provided below should assist you in deciding which combination of publications will best suit your purposes.

The Wall Street Journal. Published Monday through Friday, this is the premier business newspaper in the country and the premier spot for your advertising. However, it should be used in conjunction with other publications since not all reps are subscribers.

Aside from its prominent readership, the *Journal* has a definite cost savings feature not available in many other national publications: regional advertising. All its editions are identical in their news and fi-

* "The High Cost of Hiring," *Nation's Business,* February 1975, pp. 85–88.

nancial coverage, but advertising is sold on either a national or a regional basis and the cost is based on the number of subscribers in the area reached. Thus you can avoid paying for advertising in a marketing area that doesn't interest you.

If your rep-seeking campaign is conducted as recommended and is carried out on a region-by-region basis, the *Journal* will help you save money. A recent rate card for classified advertising shows the following per inch costs for national and regional editions:

National edition	$218.12
Eastern edition	83.30
Midwest edition	68.04
Pacific Coast edition	42.28
Southwest edition	24.50

Thus advertising for a rep in Los Angeles, for example, can be achieved by using the Pacific Coast edition at a per inch cost of $42.28 as opposed to a national rate of $218.12.

Aside from using your advertising dollar conservatively, you'll be reaching the top tier of sales reps, some of whom are not members of MANA and can't be reached except through the *Journal* or a personal contact. They don't necessarily read classified ads in other media because they usually aren't actively seeking new lines. However, just about everybody who reads the *Journal* reads its classified section. It's a barometer of business conditions. The "Manufacturing Time Open" category, for instance, used by manufacturers with excess capacity, is one of the first signals of a change in the economy. When more and more ads appear under this heading, demand for manufacturing services is clearly shrinking.

Most advertisements for reps are placed under the heading "Business Connections." An added bonus here is the occasional ad inserted by rep firms looking for specific lines. Although the mere placing of its ad in the *Journal* doesn't necessarily mean the rep firm is top-notch, chances are good that its management is a cut above average, since it's employing the top publication in an effort to locate a specific type of company to represent.

The owners of small, new, aggressive rep firms are also avid readers of the *Journal*'s classified section, so you'll be reaching both ends of the income spectrum when you place your ad here. Often a new, hungry rep firm will welcome your company with open arms where an old-line firm may not display much enthusiasm. The merits of one over another will long be argued by experienced sales managers.

Under the "Business Connections" category ads of all sizes appear, most of them too small. We'll discuss the wisdom of size later on. Both the style and the size of the ad count as attention attractors; once attention is gained, however, content is of overriding importance.

Agency Sales. This monthly magazine is the official publication of MANA; it's read by all members of that association as well as nonmember reps and sales executives of companies actively engaged in selling through reps. Strictly on a cost basis, this magazine is your best bet for reps reached per dollars spent. However, remember that these reps sell almost all varieties of manufactured goods: apparel, office supplies, auto parts, chemicals, instruments, electronic materials, and just about anything else that can be sold, including services. Thus many of the readers will not be candidates for your line.

Nevertheless, *Agency Sales* primarily reaches reps who are interested in furthering the skills and reputation of their profession. However, thousands of good reps across the country are not members of MANA and don't read *Agency Sales,* so don't advertise here to the exclusion of other publications.

The magazine has two major advertising classifications, each with a distinct purpose. The first, "Marketing Services Offered," is exclusively for rep firms (not limited to MANA members) that are actively searching for firms to represent. This section is broken down into product classifications such as building materials, instrumentation, government sales, and, of course, miscellaneous.

Reps advertising under this heading get right to the point, detailing their specialty and mentioning the exact territory they cover. The style of ads varies from straight typeset copy to fancier presentations containing a logo and even a listing of the rep's current principals. Check these columns every month under your product heading; the firms that advertise in them are aggressively trying to fill a hole in their current group of compatible lines. Yours could be the line they're seeking.

The second major advertising section is "Marketing Services Wanted." Here's the place for your ad. Again, headings are broken down into product classifications, and unless you make fur-lined breech cloths for Iroquois Indians you'll easily find a classification to suit your product. A little more imagination is exhibited in the design of the ads, but ads placed here by manufacturers are not overwhelmingly different from reps' ads.

A well-designed ad will stand out. *Agency Sales* permits display-type ads, showing the product and promotional information, whereas other publications limit ads in similar classified sections to typeset styles only. However, you'll pay a higher rate for the display ads than for the typical typeset version.

Since *Agency Sales* is about the only publication of any type devoted exclusively to the problems and challenges of the rep profession, readership is very high. Moreover, the magazine receives an inordinate amount of attention from its readers; even reps not interested in new lines will read the "Marketing Services Wanted" ads thoroughly to check out what's available in their product specialty. And occasionally you'll receive a response from a leading firm that wasn't looking for you but ran across your ad and decided to investigate your offer.

One other advertising section in *Agency Sales* may be of passing interest. "Marketing Services Directory" takes up the last few pages of the magazine; here rep firms list their name, address, and product specialties. The magazine refers to it as a "business card listing." It reminds me of "corporate image" advertising and appears to serve the purpose of saying, "While we're not in the market for a new line at present, we're established reps, and if you have something of definite interest we'll certainly be glad to hear from you."

All these sections are classified or semiclassified. One more option you have is to place a straight display advertisement in the feature section of the magazine. The rate is of course higher than for display or plain typeset ads in the "Marketing Services" sections.

Regardless of your advertising program in *Agency Sales*, you'll benefit immensely from reading this publication. Many of the articles are authored by sales managers of firms using reps, and to the credit of the editorial staff the magazine contains a lot of plain talk. No punches are pulled by either side on controversial matters, which makes for informative articles on commissions, sales strategies, and a wide range of subjects of interest to reps and sales managers.

Local newspapers. Surprisingly, a good local newspaper can be a direct route to some of the more enterprising sales reps. Always endeavoring to improve themselves by keeping abreast of what's new in the business and employment markets, these men regularly read their local papers, concentrating their interest on features that detail this information.

A particularly perceptive rep I know, who sells several highly technical products, pays close attention to the help wanted section for engineering specialists. Often these ads are quite specific about the product line of the company, enabling my friend to discover potential customers for his lines who otherwise would not have reached his attention.

If there's more than one paper in your target city, it'll pay to investigate the area of each publication's coverage if at all possible. You can write the advertising departments of the papers. They compile information of all types regarding readership, income levels of their readers, and income averages of the portions of the city where their circulation is the highest. Usually one paper will predominate in readership at the middle- to upper-income levels; this would be the preferred publication.

The newspaper itself has two sections in which you may place your advertising, one more expensive than the other but also more effective. The business section, usually included in the sports section because both features attract heavy male readership, is the most productive spot for your purpose in a local newspaper. Here you'll have to use a display ad, but it'll attract attention; and because most firms advertising for reps do so in the classified section, your ad may have little or no competition in your category. Other ads in the business section will be seeking managerial talent, which is exactly why your ad should appear here: you're trying to attract executives.

The "Help Wanted—Salesman" section, your second choice, is also a good one. Here your copy has to be very explicit because it can be buried among many other ads, most of them seeking salaried or commissioned direct employees, and unless your intent is very clear a potential rep for your line may miss it. In the classified section of a newspaper, heading and copy are doubly important.

Even though its ads are more expensive, the Sunday edition is the only one worth using for your advertising program. Sunday readership is larger. People who don't take a particular paper daily may purchase the Sunday edition because of some special features. Also, readers are much more leisurely about their reading habits on Sunday, often going through the entire paper, section by section. Contrast this with their weekday habit of scanning headlines over the morning coffee and reading only those stories that attract immediate attention. By running your ad daily in the classified section you may get a lower overall rate per inch, but it's hardly worth it. Save that money and use it for a larger ad in the Sunday issue.

Trade journals. Dollar for dollar per prospect reached for your special need, trade journals may represent the best investment for your advertising outlay, but the quality of trade journals varies so greatly that they could also represent the biggest waste of your advertising budget.

Theoretically, the trade journal offers the finest exposure possible for your ad. It's tailored to a definite group of people with a specific common interest—for the seller, the best of all possible worlds. If a golf-club manufacturer wants to reach a golfing audience, he advertises in a golfing magazine where almost every reader is a prospective customer, as opposed to a general readership magazine such as a weekly newsmagazine where one out of five readers may play the game.

The same philosophy holds true in the trade journal field. If your company makes office supplies, a trade journal in this industry will be read by reps selling office equipment, not reps selling farm tractors. What could be more ideal for your purpose?

This theory can break down in three areas: the quality of the magazine, its total circulation, and the sociological makeup of that circulation. Normally, if the quality isn't up to standard, the journal can't stay in business. So check its longevity; if the magazine is brand new, it might be better to seek out a more mature publication. Also, as a member of your specific industry, you'll have a feel for which publications you like to read. If one bores you because its articles aren't relevant or don't show thorough comprehension of the subject, chances are that it'll bore reps also.

Although important, the total-circulation figure can be misleading. If the magazine is sent free to certain personnel classifications within the industry—for example, chief engineers, purchasing agents, or sales managers—it may have a larger circulation than a paid-subscription journal, but may be inferior in quality. A journal that people will pay for must have something going for it, but for your purpose, provided the publication is well established, the makeup of its circulation may be the most important consideration in helping you decide where to place your advertisement for reps.

On request, any journal will give you a breakdown, by title, of its readers. If one journal reports a higher percentage of readers in sales positions than the others do, that would be a good sign. Your chances of reaching qualified reps should be better through this journal than through another whose readership is concentrated in more technical categories. Fortunately for your purposes, good reps are avid readers of trade journals and are often given subscriptions by their principals to help them increase their product familiarity.

One other feature to watch for in selecting the right journal is a good classified advertising section peppered with ads placed by firms wanting to hire personnel. All other qualities being relatively equal, a journal with this type of classified section would be a better choice than one in which you'd have to place a display ad.

Writing an Ad That Will Get Results

At the beginning of this chapter you read an ad that defies interpretation by anyone except an individual acquainted with the machining industry. Here's the way the ad would read if the advertiser had been willing to spend a few more dollars:

> Manufacturers' Representatives—Southeastern manufacturing company making precision machined parts of steel and brass for prominent customers needs dynamic representative organization. Write Box 234.

With this decoding, we find the ad isn't all bad. It has some good features, and with a little additional information it would stand a good chance of succeeding. It starts out in fine fashion by putting first things first. It says "Manufacturers' Representatives," a straightforward attempt to catch the attention of the person or firm the company is seeking. The ad goes on to list the company's general location, what it makes, and the purpose of the ad—to find good reps to sell its products.

However, a number of essential pieces of information are missing. These omissions are the very factors that will stimulate a rep to write you for more information.

How big is the company—five or five hundred employees?

Is the company looking for one rep organization or for several? In what geographical areas?

What is the name of the company?

Does the company have other reps, or is this its first venture into the rep field?

Is there any business in the territory? If so, are there any house accounts?

To increase the ad's effectiveness considerably, using the original format but adding information and assuming the company is just starting a rep program, this copy would attract a greater readership:

ATTENTION

MANUFACTURERS' REPRESENTATIVES

Growing Southeastern manufacturer of precision-machined steel and brass parts up to ten pounds initiating new sales program in Midwest. Reps with compatible lines can be assured of competitive pricing and prompt delivery. Exclusive territories, no house accounts. Write Ajax Products, Box 1234, Atlanta, Ga.

Here we've outlined about all this company has to offer at this point, which isn't much; but with the product line defined accurately, there's a good chance that the company will receive some response from reps who need a small precision-machined-parts source. For instance, a rep might have a good machining house that specializes in parts weighing over ten pounds, and be constantly unable to quote on smaller parts. Such a rep might well reply to this ad, but would not have bothered with the original version.

We haven't attempted to mislead in this copy. The company is obviously small, but growing. It believes it can be competitive in the Midwest, and its positive approach will seem attractive to a qualified rep. There's apparently little or no business in the area now, and the "no house accounts" advice gives further evidence of good faith, since house accounts are anathema to established reps and indicate that a company wants to have its cake and eat it too.

We also know the name of the company and the location of its plant. Many companies will omit their name and use a box number. In some instances they're trying to replace an unsatisfactory rep with another and don't want the present rep to discover that intention. The company needs publicity and secrecy, but if the ad is handled in this manner the needed publicity is negated by the need for secrecy. It's always better to discontinue relations with the old rep prior to seeking a new one. Otherwise you'll be working under an extremely difficult handicap.

Now let's take a company at the other end of the spectrum, one that has business nationally, has a rep program, and is seeking to establish a rep in a territory that appears to warrant further concentration. An ad that would catch the attention of all but the most disinterested readers might look like the one on the following page.

This ad, or a variation of it, tells your prospective rep in Nebraska and Iowa a lot of things he likes to hear about a company. You're interested in his territory. You're already working with reps. You have a specific product capability. You're competitive in his area. You have no house accounts. You'll assist him in selling your product. By frankly stating all these facts you may well attract a higher-quality response than if you had been coy about your intentions, as so many manufacturers are inclined to be, on the assumption that by telling so much in an ad they'll attract replies from unqualified reps interested only in commissions on current business.

Of course they will, but so what? There's no shortcut to good results; these reps will have to be culled from the flock through laborious effort, research, and interviews. That's the price you'll have to pay for the rewarding results you hope for in seeking the right rep for your company. In my chapter on contracts, the pros and cons of awarding commissions on existing business in an area will be probed in greater depth.

The sample ads presented here are just that. With a little imagination and an affirmative selling attitude, they can easily be tailored to your company's individual style of doing business. Pictures of your products, quotes from present reps, an offer of expenses-paid product training at your plant, and other innovative variations will all aid in your campaign to get the best rep for your company.

The point that I hope emerges from this advice is that your search for the right rep—the professional rep—should start with the same attitude that applies to selling your company's product. Although in effect you're employing a salesman, your prospective audience of candidates is limited, and so you must differentiate between the processes used in hiring a direct salesman and those used in finding a professional rep. The affirmative selling attitude is the answer. Use it to the best of your ability.

Deciding on the Size of the Ad

Based on the samples I've seen over the years, my rule of thumb would be to take the size ad you think will be most productive and double it. This may be a bit arbitrary, but it's not far from the truth.

Sometimes it seems that companies are hiding their light under a bushel—ashamed to resort to the advertising columns to find capable reps, they underplay the move. A progressive company takes a positive approach. It's proud to be expanding its marketing area. Such expansion denotes a successful and imaginative program of selling and should be shouted out loud. Let your competitors know you're on the march; they'll find out anyway. And by making a big splash you'll accomplish what this chapter is all about: attracting the guy that's going to do the best job for you.

The size of the ad you use should be adjusted to the publication it'll appear in. A two-inch, two-column ad in *Agency Sales* will compare favorably with many of the best ads in the "Marketing Services Wanted" section. However, a three-inch, two-column display ad would be much more prominent in that section. Cost difference? A hundred dollars for the two-inch ad and $150 for the three-inch ad.

The Wall Street Journal carries only one size that means anything to me: the two-inch, two-column size. Anything bigger is probably superfluous and anything smaller is much less effective. Cost? In the Midwest edition, $272.16; in the Southwest edition, $98.00. Don't worry about cost for the national edition; you shouldn't be using it. Remember, we're going to open one territory at a time.

By analyzing the size of present advertisements in the various publications you'll be using, you can easily decide on your requirements, based on the premise that your ad should be just a little bit bigger and a little bit better than the surrounding ones.

A Few Things Not to Do

Don't advertise for "aggressive" reps. Any successful rep has to be aggressive, but aggressiveness takes many forms, some highly subtle and skillful. As used in most advertising copy, "aggressive" connotes the "won't take no for an answer" type characterized by the carnival pitchman or the door-to-door peddler. I'm sure this is not what you want. An ad that contains the words "aggressive," "hard-hitting," or others with similar connotations may turn off your best prospect.

Don't ask a rep to tell you the lines he currently represents. He's not going to tell you anyway, at least not in an initial response to an ad. He doubtless has good reasons for his reticence. For example, he may currently represent one of your competitors who he wants to drop because of problems with quality, pricing, or whatever. This is strictly his own business at the beginning of negotiations, but later, when you've gained his confidence, you may properly request the information.

There's nothing wrong with asking prospective reps to state the type of lines they represent. This is a fair request, and their reply will indicate whether or not your company's product will be compatible with their existing lines. Moreover, it doesn't infringe on the rep's desire to withhold the identity of his present principals until he knows and trusts you.

To illustrate how mutually beneficial an exchange of information can be when a certain amount of trust is built up through correspondence, let me relate an experience our firm had. We were negotiating with a company that had been very honest in its initial response to an ad we placed in a trade journal. In a follow-up letter I mentioned that we represented a noncompeting firm located just a few miles from its plant. It turned out that the general manager of our principal was a personal acquaintance of the sales manager of the firm we were negotiating with. The sales manager called his friend, we were given a fine reference, and all parties benefited. We obtained a new principal and the sales manager was able to hire us secure in the knowledge that we were an established firm in our marketplace and performing to the satisfaction of at least one of our principals.

In preparing your ad copy, don't use any term for a rep other than "Manufacturers' Representative." Reps are identified by such other titles as "Sales Representatives" and "Sales Agents," but so are direct men. By sticking to "Manufacturers' Representative," which specifically denotes a self-employed commission salesman, you'll avoid confusion in the minds of your readers.

And don't fail to reply to the responses you receive from reps, particularly if you use a box number. After all, they've taken the time to write you. You owe them the courtesy of a reply, even if the volume of responses makes a form letter necessary.

So far I've refrained from suggesting that you place your advertising campaign in the hands of your advertising agency. This doesn't reflect a prejudice against advertising people, and if you have an agency by all means invite its help in developing your campaign. However, most agencies have little experience in advertising for reps, so you should set the guidelines and write the rough copy from the information in this chapter. Then bring your work in for the professional touches the agency can add to the program.

5

OTHER ROUTES
TO THE SALES REP

Personal contacts, customers,
professional recruiters

There are many ways that companies and reps come together. I've read numerous articles and books that explain how to run a sales agency, how to sell, and other essential components of a successful venture into the rep field; but none has been explicit about the most important requirement, without which there'd be no agency: how to obtain lines.

The absence of such vital advice can be credited to the realization of the writers of these articles and books that no one piece of advice is sufficiently valid to justify a firm statement. But the hardest part of becoming a rep is finding good, reputable companies to represent, companies that will be competitive and honest enough in their dealings to give the rep a chance to generate livable commissions before he runs out of money.

It's equally hard for companies to make a good connection with a rep who's right for the company—a rep who'll vigorously solicit business for the company and who works for the company's best interests rather than using the company as a vehicle toward other goals.

As I pointed out in the previous chapter, advertising is the quickest and most effective method of contacting reps, but selecting the most promising reps from the many attracted by your ads is a tough job.

You'll have to do your homework and make the most of interviews, references, and just plain hunches.

A Variety of Personal Experiences

Fortunately, we can follow other trails to find the sleepers, or the reps who might be missed by the use of conventional strategies. In examining how our own agency became associated with our principals, I thought it might be helpful to detail exactly what occurred in each case to bring about the connection.

Company A advertised in *The Wall Street Journal*, professionally outlining its product line and indicating its past successes in our area. We wrote the company, telling of our interests and background. The sales manager came down to interview candidates a few weeks later. We had a good interview and came in a strong second to a well-established firm with offices in three prominent cities in the marketing territory. The sales manager promised us that if things didn't work out with his first choice he'd give us a crack at the account. About a year and a half later, things apparently weren't working out. He flew to Dallas, and after a brief interview awarded us a contract. We've had a fine relationship ever since with this excellent company.

Company B was, and still is, a customer of ours. This firm started a small foundry when it became almost impossible to obtain castings for its product, an air tool for the automotive trade. Gradually, production increased to the point where it was economically necessary to use another type of metal part for several of the air-tool components that were formerly castings. This left the firm with the capacity to make castings for others, and sensing the opportunity, the owner set about searching for business. His efforts were successful, but he still had to concentrate on his major product, the air tool. He turned to reps and we were again second in line. But as in the case of Company A, he experienced a disappointing effort on the part of his original reps, and we've had a fine association with him ever since.

We obtained the line with Company C through a friend who had been my next-door neighbor when I lived in Illinois. Knowing he had moved to California to head a division of a well-known conglomerate, I wrote him asking if we could represent his firm in the Southwest. He replied promptly that his company was closing its operation and that he had taken an executive position with another California company.

But he gave me the ñame of the president of an excellent competitor located in the Los Angeles area, and when I phoned that gentleman he told me he was indeed interested in additional sales in our part of the country, and in fact already had some business here that we could expand on. Our negotiations were successful and we had another good firm in the fold.

Company D advertised in both the local newspapers and a trade journal. We read these publications constantly, and although the line was just a hair away from the type of products we sell, we thought it would make sense to interview for it. After a few weeks of negotiations we were awarded the line, which—despite some early doubts on the part of both parties—has come along very well.

Company E is owned by a former rep of our old Chicago firm. He had some business here but no representation. He merely said, "Have at it"—and we have.

Company F is a good, solid firm whose products I formerly bought for resale to my customers. It was well represented in our area until its rep decided to go into the manufacturing business part time. Naturally, this decision resulted in a reduced effort for the principal. A salesman for the company, recalling that we had moved here to start a rep business, had the sales manager phone us. Because of his previous business relationship with us, he sent us a contract.

Our most recently acquired principal, Company G, responded to an ad we placed in a national trade journal. We were seeking a good company to fill a gap in our line of compatible products. My partner traveled to Chicago and was interviewed by the sales manager. The agreement we concluded has resulted in a profitable association for both the company and our agency.

These contacts, each made in a different manner, took place over a period of *five* years, which is why I've emphasized patience in planning a rep sales program. Good, profitable associations simply don't happen overnight; nor do they occur as a result of any one program, as demonstrated by the varied experiences our agency went through before obtaining a well-rounded, compatible group of principals.

I'm sure any rep you talk to will agree that a variety of planned, unplanned, and accidental developments led to his linkups with principals. Rather than bank on providence or some ethereal breakthrough, you should explore the well-known avenues that complement your advertising campaign.

Ask Your Customers for Recommendations

Unless you already have a customer or two in the area, you can skip this piece of advice. If the customer you do have has a purchasing agent whose judgment you've learned to respect, you can begin by consulting him.

You may be surprised to learn that not all purchasing agents are anxious to recommend a specific rep. This attitude is really to their credit. It means they don't want to obligate their company or themselves. If a purchasing agent singles out one rep for hearty endorsement, that could place the P.A. in an awkward position. He may suppose that if you sign up his candidate you'll be expecting more than your share of his business. Because of this, some purchasing people refrain from offering any suggestions.

Fortunately, many purchasing agents name four or five reps they respect, and let you be the judge of their capabilities. This can be a profitable course for both parties. If you receive several suggestions, you should by all means follow them up. This not only is a good method of obtaining reps but will show your respect for the purchasing agent's willingness to aid you.

Professional purchasing agents are skilled judges of salesmen's abilities, but beware of the purchasing man who plays favorites. This type of buyer could hurt you. In addition to performing a disservice to his company, he can lead you astray with his recommendations, and you may wind up with a rep who sells well at only one or two firms. And even here his success may be due to his status as a favorite bar buddy or golfing companion to the buyer. If the buyer leaves his firm, your business could disappear with him.

One more hint. If you have several customers in the new area and two or more purchasing people include the same rep among their recommendations, you should definitely attempt to interview the rep so recommended.

Other Sales Managers Can Help You

Through clubs, associations, and mutual business acquaintances, you probably know a number of sales managers in related but noncompeting industries. Here's a fine source for new reps. For instance, when I was employed by a Chicago area firm, we had reps who worked for three or four other forging firms whose end products were different from ours and different from each other's but were nevertheless forgings. Their ability to take care of any customer's forging needs made these reps valuable salesmen, for both their principals and their customers.

The items a rep handles need not be as closely related as these forging products. Apparel, for instance, offers a wide assortment of noncompeting items from men's pants to ladies bras, but reps handling various apparel lines call on many of the same firms, if not the same buyer. Plastic goods, building materials, hardware items, and an endless number of broad product categories include numerous specialized lines within their purview.

The more sales managers you know within a general industry, the more opportunities you have to find a seasoned rep for your firm. This is one of the most dependable modes for contacting good reps, since an effective rep for another company in your general field has a better than even chance for success with your product. However, there are some real pitfalls here for both your company and your rep.

The biggest danger—and a common problem—is the likelihood of overlapping products. For example, the case of the reps handling four forging lines: Our company made custom forgings weighing between about 8 and 300 pounds, and several of these reps worked with manufacturers producing custom forgings weighing from one to 15 pounds. Since our specialty was in the heavier forgings, we put up with the minor annoyance of this overlap at the lower end of the weight scale because it was to our advantage to have reps capable of offering a complete range of forgings to potential customers.

Thus, before plunging headlong into exchanges of information with other sales managers, be sure there are no areas of conflict that would create misunderstandings. If these occur, talk them out frankly to see if a compromise can be reached to everyone's satisfaction.

An examination of this arrangement from the rep's point of view reveals another set of circumstances. If several of the rep's principals have sales managers who are in casual contact with each other, the rep becomes concerned about his security. Most sales managers make decisions about rep policies on their own, and base these decisions on the results they see in the field.

Still, a sales manager disenchanted with a particular rep can pass along these feelings to the other sales managers. Even though the disenchantment may stem from trivial personality differences between the sales manager and the rep and have nothing to do with end results, the other sales managers may subconsciously question their own positive feelings toward the rep in question. Knowing this, reps are reluctant to line up with a coterie of well-acquainted sales managers, so don't be surprised if one of your friend's successful reps finds it convenient not to join your rep group.

Despite these possible conflicts, many such arrangements work out very well. I'm sure a moment's thought will bring to mind a number of your own business acquaintances with whom an exchange of information can be mutually beneficial.

Your Current Reps Know the Field

Reps are getting to know each other very well these days, thanks to more sales meetings by principals and MANA activities and seminars. By responding to an ad we placed, one of our present principals discovered that we knew one of his top reps. The sales manager phoned the rep and we received a good reference.

If you currently have a good rep group, these men will put you in touch with reps throughout the country. Though they may not have firsthand knowledge of the actual ability of these acquaintances, they'll be aware of many other factors of importance: how long they've been with other principals, what types of firms they represent, and perhaps even some of their major customers.

We've had many such cross references over the years but have always been careful to confine our remarks to the actual facts. Simply because a rep is a good friend and an effective representative for his other principals is not reason enough to tell a sales manager that the rep will be good for him and his company. Even the rep involved doesn't know if this is true. As Lee Walters correctly puts it, "There is absolutely no way to know in advance how a line is going to turn out." * But most other attributes can be freely discussed, and we never hesitate to tell our companies' sales managers of other good reps we know—if they ask!

* Pauline Neff, "Lee Walters Associates Makes Every Day Count," *Agency Sales*, June 1973, pp. 5–7.

He's Somewhere in the MANA Directory

All members of MANA, over 4,000 of them, are listed in the annual directory (available to nonmembers for $20). The directory can be obtained from the Manufacturers' Agents National Association, 3130 Wilshire Boulevard, Suite 509, Los Angeles, California 90010. Reps are listed alphabetically, by territory, and by product line. But membership in MANA doesn't automatically transform an ordinary garden-variety rep into a professional manufacturers' representative—that's a lot to ask for $65, the annual dues—so don't assume that if you find a rep in the directory with lines compatible to yours, your prayers have been answered.

Now that I've made this disclaimer, let me add that in my opinion the overwhelming majority of firms listed in the directory are made up of top-notch businessmen. They've joined MANA for a number of reasons: to help upgrade the profession, to learn from their peers, to be part of an association that will represent them forcefully in many arenas, and to help them find good principals.

Issued every spring, the directory has several purposes, but the prime reason for its existence is to bring reps and companies together. To supplement their regular standardized listing, some rep firms place modest advertisements. The ad is usually located in the vicinity of the firm's listing and enables it to give more facts about its agency. Since the information in the standard listing is necessarily limited, you'll find these ads quite informative. Reps who advertise in the directory are looking for lines; that may make them better prospects for you.

I recommend against advertising for reps in the MANA directory. Since the directory appears only once a year, your message may get a little old and your needs may have changed considerably before next year's edition is published.

Check Inquiries from Reps

If your firm has any reputation at all in its industry, you'll receive letters from reps inquiring about the possibility of their representing you in their selling area. These inquiries should be given very careful attention. These reps write you for definite reasons.

1. They may have several lines complementary to yours and wish to add the products of your company to fill a void.
2. They may have recently lost a line similar to yours and have business without any place to send it.
3. They may have one or two customers urgently looking for an additional source of your product.
4. They may have recently formed their agency and be looking for lines compatible with their experience and product knowledge.

The usual lack of affirmative response to these inquiries is explained by their unfortunate timing. Seldom are you actively looking for a rep in the rep's territory at the exact time you receive his letter. This is understandable, but what you do with his letter can adversely affect your search for a good rep in that area at a later date. Your normal reply to the rep is that either you're presently represented in the area or you have no current need for representation. It closes with: "If the situation should change, we'll be sure to get in touch with you." And that's usually that. The carbon copy goes into a file somewhere and is promptly forgotten.

While the timing of these letters won't improve simply because you may now be more conscious of their importance, you have everything to gain by developing a file that will be readily available for future reference. Who knows, three months from now one of your better local customers may announce removal of his operations to Alva, Oklahoma, and you'll be frantically searching your files for the letter received a few months back from a rep in Tulsa, and you may not find it.

When you receive a particularly impressive inquiry from a rep in a marketing area you're not quite ready to enter, reconsider. If you're even remotely thinking about that area, this may be one occasion where you should jump the gun—but of course only if the rep is truly exceptional and you can compete with other firms selling there. If you delay entering the market until you're absolutely and finally ready, your company may have lost the one good rep the territory offers. He may have been urgently trying to locate a manufacturer of your product, and your delay may have forced him to sign with a less promising competitor. Although this is contrary to my previous suggestion about not entering a marketing area before you're prepared, you must not miss a rare opportunity simply because it doesn't exactly coincide with your planned timing.

Professional Recruiters May Be Your Answer

This is a field that has been sadly overlooked by the reputable search firms. If you've had any experience at all with professional recruiters—or headhunters as they're known in the trade—you're familiar with the number of firms in this business and the fees they receive for enticing executives to leave a warm, comfortable position with one firm for a warmer and more comfortable position with another firm, usually at an attractive increase in pay.

Servicing the rep field may never have occurred to these search firms because basically, as salesmen, we're classified with the Indians instead of the Chiefs—perhaps their corporate clients would be reluctant to spend $10,000 to $15,000 to find a good Indian. But why not? A rep with an annual income of $100,000 to $200,000 is not rare—I know several in this bracket—and it would be worth $15,000 to the right firm with the right product to enlist such a go-getter's services. With interest in selling through reps increasing—particularly among larger corporations—this appears to be a fertile field for search firms with initiative.

I know of only two small firms that serve this field. They've done the job effectively for a number of years, although their search methods differ from those of a true search firm. The first company is a one-man operation located on the Eastern seaboard. Over the years this man has compiled a file on rep firms and the type of products they handle. He approaches companies needing reps in specific areas and for a fee agrees to find a suitable rep for them.

He then sends qualified reps a short description of the firm and its products and usually includes the company's literature or brochures. The interested rep is asked to reply, giving the names of his current principals as well as the names of personal contacts at six of his customers. The gentleman then checks out these references, makes up a file on each rep, and presents the information to his clients, who arrange for interviews with the reps.

The one client interview we had through this firm was with the president and sales manager of a very fine casting company. The firm obviously had a complete file on us. That interview took place in the formative days of our agency, but now, in the cold light of day and with a group of excellent principals and equally good customers, we think twice about revealing personal customer contacts that have taken us years to develop. We have absolutely no quarrel with this recruiter and have no reason to suspect for a minute that this confidential information is released to anyone but his interested clients. However, we'd rather not divulge such vital information until a prospective principal has shown a particular and sincerely convincing interest in us.

The second firm also has a good file on reps nationwide but handles its search in a slightly different fashion. A comprehensive fact sheet on its client company is mailed to reps. It tells about the company and in some cases sets up specific classifications or parameters for reps required by the client, for example, insistence on multi-personnel, technically competent firms. Nonqualifying reps thus can avoid a lot of futile correspondence; the search firm merely puts interested parties in touch with each other.

For a $20 yearly fee to the search firm, reps receive their fact sheet several weeks before nonprivileged reps do, and so get a timing advantage over their peers. Working through this company also allows a rep to initiate negotiations with a prospective principal without revealing any intimate details of his agency until he's ready to do so.

Both these search firms have been in business for many years and evidently are sufficiently successful in their efforts to continue to operate. From time to time, enterprising individuals have made feeble attempts to organize a marketplace where reps and companies could meet, for a fee; but these endeavors have seldom prospered, and after a year or two no more is heard of them.

There's of course no harm in working with one of these firms. They'll relieve you of much of your detail work for a reasonable fee. But they may be operating from some of the same listings that are available to you, such as the MANA directory. Also, some of the very reps you're seeking may have the same doubt we profess—a disinclination to reveal the names of personal contacts at customers' plants—and therefore would not respond to the recruiter's inquiry.

For the busy sales manager, or the small firm whose owner also serves as sales manager, use of a professional recruiter or search firm might be a practical move. However, I believe that more sophisticated companies, using the methods described in this book, can conduct a more efficient and controlled search than can professional recruiters currently serving the field.

Trade Shows Are Always a Possibility

At a trade show held in Dallas during the 1970 recession, the president of a metal-stamping firm exhibiting there told me he talked with more reps seeking his line than customers wanting to buy his products. Although he was exaggerating to emphasize the lack of business, he was definitely approached by a number of rep firms eager to inspect the quality of his products first hand. Also, his company's willingness to fund an exhibit at a time when his competitors were retrenching and slashing advertising and promotional budgets favorably impressed the progressive reps who spent their own money to attend the show.

My partner and I never miss a good trade show in our territory, for two reasons. One, we're always searching for potential customers for our companies' products; and two, we keep a lookout for companies who may desire representation in our area for lines compatible with ours. In addition, we usually exhibit at one or more trade shows each year, and our principals are happy to help us out with expenses, signs, and booth personnel. Our major thrust here is to sell our companies' products, but we've had some interesting discussions with prospective principals who find it hard to believe that a rep firm will spend its own money on sales promotion.

By becoming a regular exhibitor at regional and national shows, not only will you stimulate interest in your product, but you may find one or two excellent reps who attend these shows to increase their knowledge and add to their selling effectiveness.

Through advertising and the sources reviewed in this chapter, you'll be able to engage in a comprehensive search for the reps you need in your national or regional marketing program. As you can see from the multitude of sources at your command, a productive rep-gathering program will take time and money. But if you're serious about wanting a high-caliber staff of reps, you'll make this investment. Time, money, and energy expended now—as with any good investment—will return substantial long-term profits later on.

6

THE INTERVIEW

Separating the men from the boys

If everything goes according to plan, your advertising program and the other sources suggested in the preceding pages should produce many inquiries from promising candidates seeking to represent you. The response may in fact be overwhelming and somewhat frightening. Frightening because the replies you receive must serve as the basis for selecting the reps you'll consider worth interviewing. This can be a formidable task.

Narrowing the Field of Candidates

Two of our principals received 77 and 44 responses respectively in their campaign to find a sales agency to represent them in our area. In a situation like this, knowing which replies to eliminate quickly is your first priority.

Handwritten letters. One of the most successful reps I know wrote his letters by hand for years, but he's truly the exception. Letters that aren't typed show either lack of real interest or lack of professionalism. Unless there's some clue that the writer is an exceptional individual, handwritten replies can usually be discarded.

Noninformation replies. If a rep merely states that he's interested and asks for further information without telling you anything at all

...ncy, he isn't showing much genuine interest, unless ...en exceedingly sketchy in your ad—in which case you'll re- ...a number of replies of this type. The rep who responds should ...ve the courtesy and intelligence to give you a brief rundown on his agency and the types of lines he handles.

Overeager replies. The rep who wants your line without hearing more about your firm and its products is not a good risk. He can't possibly know whether or not he wants your line without fully understanding your firm's policies and products. Your company, its products, and its successes may be so well known that the rep's request is legitimate, but this is infrequently the case. A more plausible explanation for his blind and reckless faith is that the rep is new and inexperienced and is attempting to gather many lines as quickly as possible. While a man showing that much enthusiasm shouldn't be dropped from consideration immediately, I'd put him in the "pending" file for the moment.

Replies promising prompt business. This is tempting; it's somewhat like listening to the stockbroker with a hot tip on a fast-breaking stock. But your chances are better with the hot-tip stockbroker than with the rep who promises immediate orders. This adventurer will tell you he has customers who can hardly wait to force orders on him as soon as you give him the line, whereas a reputable rep goes after a line only when he's quite certain that he can sell the product to his customers. His past experiences temper his enthusiasm; he realizes you're not yet a proven supplier of quality goods, at the right price, at least as far as his customers are concerned, so he won't make any wild promises. And even when he does become convinced that your company can perform in his area, he'll show only cautious optimism until he has actually moved some of your products.

By a process of elimination, using the preceding criteria and good common sense, you can narrow your prospective field to no more than ten reps. More than this can be confusing when you must conduct extensive interviews with all your potential reps over a two- or three-day period. Too many interviews can lead to mental exhaustion and the risk of an unfortunate choice.

Planning and Conducting Your Interviews

Once you've chosen your group it's essential that you be professional in planning your interviews, since all your previous effort and expense can be wasted by an ill-conceived or hastily set up program. Several suggestions are offered here for your consideration when planning interviews with prospective reps; these will augment your carefully planned strategy to guarantee the wise choice of a new rep.

Interviews should be conducted in the reps' area. Unless you've narrowed your choice to two or three reps, in which case interviews can be combined with plant familiarization, arrange to hold your interviews in the reps' territory. A good, centrally located motel is usually convenient, but trying to conduct an interview in a small motel room cramps everyone's style, and so if a suite is available, by all means take advantage of it. The spaciousness and informal atmosphere of a suite or sitting room will put both you and your guests at ease and promote a more open, friendly, and informative discussion.

Schedule interviews intelligently. The beginning or the end of the workweek will find most reps available for an interview. The middle of the week will find most of them out in the territory and scheduling will be more difficult. Many sales managers plan Thursday and Friday meetings with Saturday left open for a second interview for promising reps. Only prior commitments could make a rep who's interested in your line object to a Saturday interview.

Interviews should be scheduled about an hour apart. This allows about 45 minutes for a fairly thorough interview and gives you a 15-minute breathing spell between interviews. No rep likes to leave the room just as another is entering it.

Exceptions can be planned for in advance. A luncheon date or the last interview of the day can be reserved for a rep who's especially promising.

Bring along a business associate. It's unusual for a sales manager to hire a direct salesman without first having the applicant meet several people within the organization. This personal contact is not practical when hiring reps, since the interview takes place away from the home office, sometimes many hundreds of miles away. Thus the assistant sales manager or some other executive who may be working with the rep in the future should accompany you if possible. I'm suggesting, not dilution of the decision-making responsibility, but a more objective decision based on the impressions and nuances that can be gained from hearing another viewpoint.

Prior to holding your first interview in an area, it would be wise to form a composite picture of the type of person you'll be talking with. Usually he'll be a mature, successful salesman who at one time probably held an executive position similar to yours. His income is likely to be good, but he's seeking to improve it, or he wouldn't be there. He's had many such interviews before, and because he's self-employed and time is money, he'll be direct in both his answers and his questions.

You'll find him cordial—but anxious, as you are, to discover as quickly as possible whether there's the possibility of a mutual advantage in working together. He's not interested in going through the procedures often required in hiring a direct salesman—for example, psychological testing, physical examinations, and references from past employers—but at the right time he should be pleased to give you references from his other principals.

After getting through the initial social amenities, a good practice is to give the rep a five-minute thumbnail sketch of your company, its products and its personnel, and why you're interested in good representation in his area. You can then ask him for a short history of his firm.

One sales manager opened an interview with us by asking, "And how much business can you dig up for us down here in Texas?" Having only a slight knowledge of his firm and very little appreciation of his firm's competitiveness or quality, we simply said, "We have no idea." That wasn't the answer he was looking for, but it was an honest one. The opening briefing can avoid embarrassment to both parties and can clear the air for a good interview.

Questions You Must Ask the Rep

The opening exchange of information will bring several questions to your mind, and you should ask them. However, an already prepared, informal list of several probing questions for all the reps to answer will provide an objective standard for comparing their merits.

How long have you been in business? There's no "right" answer to this question, but the length of time an agency has been in business can be relevant to the type of selling that works best for your company in current marketing areas. For instance, if you need volume orders from large companies, you may find that older, established reps who have developed business and social relationships within this type of company will best suit your purposes. They may work with fewer customers, but these few may be sold in depth because of the rep's intimate knowledge of their personnel, their policies, and their methods of buying.

However, if something you make must be sold to many firms to meet your goals—for example, plant maintenance supplies or office machinery—then a younger agency will be more likely to make the number of daily new calls necessary to establish your product in the territory. Because it depends on quick income to get past its breakeven point, a younger agency has to stay constantly active in the field to develop the customers that will provide this needed income.

This is not to say that an older agency won't work hard toward finding new customers; but unless your potential business warrants hiring an additional salesman to make missionary calls exclusively, the older agency will tend to depend more on current customers for a substantial portion of its business.

How many lines do you handle? At a MANA seminar for manufacturers and sales reps—reported in the August 1972 issue of *Agency Sales*—one manufacturer complained vigorously about a rep who was soliciting his line but who already had 23 others. The rep told him that four of the lines contributed most of his commissions, ten contributed occasionally, and the other nine were marginal.

The manufacturer had a right to be concerned, but such an operation is not unusual in some areas of selling. For instance, reps selling to retail outlets or automotive jobbers will carry a substantial number of lines. Many of them will not have universal appeal because of the public's limited need for the product, but by selling through 25 to 50 reps some manufacturers may receive a tidy income. Their reps, in turn, may benefit by being of service to their customers, which can lead to sales of other, higher-volume items.

As a rule, however, 23 lines would represent a pretty diversified group. When your prospective reps have ten or more, you should inquire about their reasons for such diversity, but don't hesitate to become the twelfth or fifteenth line if your product is complementary to one of the rep's most profitable lines—it could be worth it to you. As a matter of academic interest, reps participating in our RepSurvey carried an average of nine lines.

Thus, it's not the *number* of his lines that makes a rep good for you; it's your understanding of why he has a certain number that is of most importance.

What is your geographical selling area? To cite a geographical oddity, one that tends to cause headaches when awarding territories, look at the Cleveland-Pittsburgh area. A rep based in Cleveland will normally cover the entire state of Ohio, but will also venture into western Pennsylvania, including Pittsburgh, because of its proximity to Cleveland and the potential business there. Another rep based in Pittsburgh may cover most of Pennsylvania, but will venture into eastern Ohio, again because of its proximity and the amount of potential business the area offers.

You can visualize the complications inherent in working out a suitable arrangement, particularly if both reps are desirable for your company. Compromise is not unusual, however, especially if all parties stand to benefit from a territory plan that considers the major selling area of each rep. But if it appears that the Ohio rep is much stronger than his Pittsburgh neighbor, or if the Ohio market is one of your better selling territories, then you could justifiably award the geography in question to the Cleveland rep.

There are puzzling inconsistencies in what would otherwise appear to be a sensible division of territories by states alone. For example, New Orleans, located on the gulf in Louisiana, is home base for excellent reps who service their entire state. Yet many companies will award Shreveport, Louisiana, to Dallas reps because Shreveport, 320 miles from New Orleans, lies adjacent to the East Texas selling area of Tyler, Marshall, Kilgore, and Longview, all normally serviced by Dallas reps.

A discussion of the MANA-recommended territory divisions, including a map, appears in the next chapter.

How many and what type customers do you have? A few quite successful reps specialize in fields that involve a minimum number of customers, such as discount-store chains. Here volume is tremendous, and these specialists may work with one or two buyers who are responsible for purchasing for a hundred or more stores. If your product is sold directly to independents in the retail field, this is not the type of rep for you.

Other reps solicit business from one industry exclusively and may have 10 or 20 customers, but only in that industry. If your product is sold not only to that industry but to others, you may want to consider using two separate reps. For instance, we represented a firm that made a commodity for general industry and for manufacturers of mobile homes. Salesmen who call on mobile-home builders usually specialize in that industry because the intense competition demands almost day-to-day contact. It was therefore perfectly logical for our principal to use our selling abilities in the general industry market and to hire another rep to call only on buyers in the mobile-home industry. Appointing either of us exclusively would have resulted in our principal not realizing his maximum potential in our area.

For a company with a product line of broad appeal, the rep with a good number of customers in diversified industries is of course the best bet. Naturally, the quality of those customers is important, and if you reach a productive point in your negotiations with a particular rep, he should be willing to supply several customer references; these should definitely be requested.

How many sales people do you have? Whether you go with a single-man or a multi-man agency can be decided by the size of the territory, the potential gross sales, and the different types of industries to which your product can be sold. So many combinations are possible here that it would be foolish to offer specific guidelines, but some information about the different types of rep organizations that you'll encounter may be helpful.

The true single-man firm may be owned by an older established rep or a newcomer to the business. The established rep probably has a well-defined selling ritual, which encompasses calls on current customers and a few on potential customers. The newcomer should be making more cold calls. The effectiveness of either type of rep depends on the man, his territory, and your product.

The multi-man agency will normally be an outgrowth of the single-man agency, for several reasons. The originator's successful selling tactics may have brought him so much business that he's incapable of physically taking his volume past a certain point. At this plateau he may bring in an employee or a partner—more likely an employee, since his success limits his need for additional capital and it's to his advantage to retain financial control of his agency. As he continues to grow he may hire additional sales people, some of whom will live in other parts of his territory to reduce travel expense and provide more effective servicing of customers.

In another case, a man may be trying to cover too much territory and consequently hit the high spots only, leaving many potential customers undiscovered. He may merge with another rep who has the same problem in a distant part of the territory. By working together, the two reps are able to canvass their respective areas more thoroughly and do a better job for their principals.

Another quite common type of multi-man agency is not an individual entity but consists of two or more reps who agree to work on a split commission basis. For instance, Texas and Oklahoma are viewed by most manufacturers as a single territory; yet Tulsa, Oklahoma, is approximately 800 miles from Brownsville, Texas, making it impossible for one man to offer any degree of effective coverage in that territory.

In this situation, a rep in Houston seeking your line will contact other independent reps in Dallas and Tulsa and work out an arrangement whereby the other two reps handle your line on a split commission basis in their areas, with the seller of the goods receiving the larger share. The Houston rep, in turn, will offer this same selling service for the Dallas and Tulsa reps.

These three reps may present themselves to the sales manager as a three-man agency, when in reality they're actually three separate agencies. This is not necessarily a surreptitious arrangement, but unless you investigate a multi-man agency thoroughly you may be joining up with such a group without knowing it. While this type of organization will give you broader coverage, it has some drawbacks.

Each rep will establish his priorities as far as principals are concerned. All three may have several principals in common, but may also have separate principals that suit their individual territory or characteristics. This can mean an uneven performance for you, resulting in excellent sales in one portion of the territory and total neglect in another.

If this happens, what do you do? You're reluctant to lose the rep or two who are showing promise, but the third rep, whom you haven't heard from in months, may have the portion of the territory with the most potential. Since the three are loosely tied together, it's hard to terminate one without the possibility of alienating the other two.

The other possibility is that your disenchantment with the one rep, when transmitted to the successful reps, will cause dissension within their ranks. For this reason, associations of individual reps are tenuous propositions at best, and unless groups of this type can prove several years of successful operation, you should approach a contract with them with extreme caution.

What are your growth plans? Occasionally you'll be confronted by a rep looking for a line to replace a lost one. This in itself is commendable and can result in solid benefits for your company, depending on the reason for the rep's termination of his previous line. If it was because of poor sales for an undistinguished company with no interest in the market, or a merger, or a new sales manager, he may be your man.

However, if he's concerned only with replacing his lost line and shows no interest in other profitable lines, he may be well satisfied with his present income level and have no desire or need to improve it. This is an unusual attitude for a rep. As noted in an earlier chapter, one of a rep's characteristics is his pursuit of ultimate financial security—an unobtainable goal. But despite this drive on the part of most reps, one occasionally appears who is happy at a certain income level and is concerned only with maintaining that income, not increasing it.

While many of us envy someone who can maintain his peace of mind at such a plateau, a rep with such an outlook is not an ideal candidate for you. By soliciting orders from customers of his previous similar line he may at first bring you more business than you had, but having replaced his lost business he may lack motivation for further activity on your behalf.

It pays, therefore, to ask your prospective reps about their goals and plans for future growth. Those replying with vague assurances of ever-increasing efforts should be questioned more closely about their actual plans—more sales people, more promotional effort, or specific five- and ten-year goals? For instance, if yours is a manufacturing firm interested in profitable expansion, a rep with the same goals for his agency as yours for your company is by far a more logical choice than a rep who's happy with maintaining his status quo.

What are your plans for agency continuity? Presupposing that any agreement you reach with a rep is based on an association that will last forever, your natural inclination is to go with a rep firm peopled by younger men. However, as a result of your interview, an older, more mature rep will often appear to be your best bet. If he's in the 50- to 60-year age bracket, you may find yourself wondering about the wisdom of your choice, particularly if he's closer to 60. But while reps much older than 60 are still very effective, as we grow older our remaining selling days become fewer. Therefore, if you're inclined to hire the older rep, it's in your best interest to ask if he has a younger associate or a definite commitment to a plan for the continuance of his agency in the event of his retirement or premature death.

If he already has a younger associate, that man should be present during the interview. If you're actively interested in hiring this rep, and he hasn't brought his associate to the interview, you should insist on meeting the younger man before offering a contract. He may turn out to be a dud brought on board to give false credence to the rep's declaration of sincere desire to provide agency continuity.

A good example of a firm that has placed a priority on continuity is the George T. Cook Company of Shawnee Mission, Kansas. This agency was established by George T. Cook in 1910, a long time ago for the rep business. With unusual foresight, the founder and his successors brought in Cook Jordan and George Seymour in 1955, and today this firm is as vital and progressive as it was at its inception. Also, not content with selling exclusively to the railroad industry, its original market, the agency diversified into the general industrial market shortly after 1955 and grew sufficiently to warrant opening a branch office in 1967 in Wichita, Kansas.

Questions the Rep Should Ask You

Up to now you've been asking all the questions, but before the interview is concluded the rep should have several questions of his own. He needs to know a few particulars about your company in addition to those you gave him in the original briefing at the beginning of the interview. Here are some of the questions he may ask and the reasons why he's interested in your answers.

If you had a previous rep in the area, why is he no longer representing you? The rep is trying to discover what your performance standards are—whether your company is fickle in its hiring and firing of reps or simply picked a lemon the first time around. Some sales managers expect sales results to be consistent in all marketing areas, but hardworking, effective reps may produce widely varying results in different competitive situations. Unrealistic company standards can scare off a good rep who suspects you don't understand the potential for your company in his area.

For instance, one of our lines sells better in Oklahoma than in Texas. The demand for this product is great in Texas, but for some unfathomable reason the competition there is much more severe. To an inexperienced sales manager it would appear that we're concentrating our efforts in Oklahoma and neglecting Texas, because our Oklahoma sales are much higher than our Texas sales. A knowledgeable sales manager must understand the differing competitive climates in different territories and revise company sales expectations to reflect these differences.

On the other hand, if the rep being interviewed knows that your previous rep in the area was ineffective or had other lines that were not sufficiently complementary to yours, he can readily appreciate your reasons for wanting to change.

Do you have any business in the area, and if so, how did you obtain it? Your reaction to this question is likely to be a lively suspicion that the rep is primarily interested in how much income he's going to receive from your present accounts rather than how he can help you gain more. However, if you're interviewing a reputable rep, there are a couple of legitimate reasons for his asking this question.

1. You may have tried to convince him that your company will be extremely competitive in his territory, but if you have little or no business there he may think you really don't know whether or not you can compete. And it's quite expensive for a rep to pioneer a line for several months only to find that your company can't deliver competitive prices.

2. If your present business was obtained through your reputation, a direct-mail program, or occasional visits, he knows that by good local representation the volume can be increased.

One of our principals had at one time covered our territory with a direct salesman. However, the territory was too large, and eventually the company withdrew him from the area. Except for sporadic visits by the sales manager, the territory was not worked for three years; yet when it was turned over to us, complete with commissions, our enthusiasm was unbridled. Because of a good direct-mail program and delivery of a quality product, the company had maintained most of its accounts and business was still very good. We knew that with our additional coverage business would get even better, and our hunch has paid off.

Do you have other reps? The first rep with any company is in a tough position. The company has no previous experience on which to base its assessment of the rep's results. Whether he's held in high esteem or low regard depends on the extent of the company's understanding of the representative way of selling. A firm with a well-established rep force will convince the prospective rep of its ability to supply him with the help he needs in soliciting business, whereas a company lacking experience with other reps must launch a massive effort to orient company personnel to the procedures necessary for smooth operation of correspondence and other phases of a rep program.

Other questions the rep may ask are presented in Chapter 3.

Deciding on the Right Rep

The interviews will result in some very definite opinions on the positive merits of one or more reps. If one rep stands out head and shoulders above the rest, he should be asked for references and informed that he's in strong contention for the line. If two or more appear to be excellent prospects, a second interview with each is advisable.

This second interview can be decisive, since questions may have surfaced during interviews with some reps that were left unasked in interviews with other reps. For example, the last rep you interviewed may have touched on his relationship with a group of companies that offer a tremendous potential for your product. A second interview with a rep who impressed you earlier but had not mentioned this group will give him a chance to explain his own contact with those same companies. References should be checked, customers should be contacted, and even the financial strength of the candidates should be assessed. Normally, however, the second interview will make your best choice fairly obvious.

If you're able to make a decision while still in town, call your first choice and arrange to meet him for contract negotiations. At this point it's best not to notify the second and third choices that they haven't been chosen. Contract negotiations are the most delicate phase of hiring a rep, and agreements are not always reached. A territorial conflict, a company policy of withholding selected.house accounts, or an unacceptable commission rate structure may make the first choice decide not to sign. By not notifying other reps of your decision until a contract has been signed, they remain candidates in the event that a contract with the first choice is not signed.

One more word of caution. The average company sales manager is a dynamic personality. To reach his present position he has had to work hard, compromise, smile when he didn't want to, and stay alive in a very competitive profession. This calls for exceptional ability and a public appearance of sparkling dynamism.

Not infrequently, a sales manager unfamiliar with the rep profession will be subconsciously seeking an alter ego among the reps he interviews and may be disappointed by the personalities he encounters in our business. Even though a successful rep has to have many of the sales manager's attributes—after all, he's a manager too—a dynamic personality may not be included in his repertoire. He no longer has to walk the tightrope of company politics, he doesn't have to sparkle at industry conventions, and he doesn't have to provide a constant stimulus to an indifferent sales force or a widely varied collection of sales reps. He does have to sell, though, and needs to concentrate on the characteristics necessary to accomplish this purpose.

The difference in roles between sales manager and rep makes for a difference in their selling personalities. When the sales manager recognizes this, the panic he may begin to experience at the outset of his initial rep interviews should evaporate.

7

CONTRACT TIME

Who goes where, who gets what?

A fair portion of contract and territory negotiations will take place during your preliminary and final interviews. For the sake of clarity and the needed emphasis on the contract portion of your negotiations, contract details will be covered in a separate chapter.

Thrash Out the Details Immediately

Too often after having made his choice, a sales manager's parting words to the rep are, "I'll have a contract in the mail to you within a week or so." This is a mistake, because differing interpretations of various clauses often surface later and lead to misunderstandings. Only by going over the contract with the rep in person can the sales manager explain ambiguous clauses and clarify those that appear not to be in agreement with the verbal understanding. Though it may seem like a bothersome extra chore at the time, handling the details long distance later may prove more difficult than thrashing them out on the spot.

Also, there's always the slight chance that certain disagreements may cause you to terminate negotiations with your chosen rep. Discovering this a week or two later, when you're back at the office tend-ing to other urgent matters, would not only be annoying but might necessitate expensive re-interviews of other candidates.

The "handshake" agreement. No matter how impressed you are with your prospective rep, there's no room in modern business for the "handshake" agreement. Yet it's not unusual for an owner of a smaller firm to insist on an association based only on a "handshake." This is understandable; in most cases it demonstrates the conviction of the owner that his reps have high moral standards and feel a kinship with him, and in the past many long-standing relationships were established on this basis. Today, however, it's incongruous for a sales manager to offer a "handshake" contract—even though at the bidding of his boss. All meaning is lost because the very essence of such an arrangement is mutual trust between two men. The sales manager is a third party, and such an agreement—reached without the rep ever having met the owner—lacks the old meaning.

A "handshake" agreement also lessens the sales manager's ability to direct a viable program within the kinds of strong parameters that are offered by a contractual arrangement. Any steps taken to enforce company policies with regard to reps' actions, policies, or terminations can be questioned by the reps and can even lead to lawsuits.

Another, more common deterrent for the rep to this type of informal agreement is the increasing number of businesses being sold to conglomerates. How or why the business has changed hands is not of intense interest to the company's reps, but the new owner who now confronts them is of vital concern. Too many reps have received a phone call from an unfamiliar corporate official announcing immediate termination of the relationship with no accruing commissions or further considerations.

Even without such jolts brought on by new ownership, misunderstandings of an ordinary nature are rife in "handshake" agreements. Controversy can erupt over commission rates if an owner arbitrarily decides they're too high and changes them overnight. Territories that have been defined by verbal agreement only are subject to various interpretations by either party; New York, for instance, could mean New York City to one party and the state of New York to the other.

Confusion over commissions can arise when a product is sold in one rep's territory and shipped into another's area. Also, does the rep receive a commission on rejected goods? In the event of termination, are commissions paid on all orders on the books at time of termination? Some business owners can be capricious and will sometimes terminate a rep on a whim rather than for solid business reasons—and then rub salt in the wound by refusing to pay accrued commissions.

These and many more possibilities for potential misunderstanding can be covered by a good contract. Remembering painful experiences resulting from "handshake" agreements, veteran reps will have nothing to do with them. Neither should you.

The sample contract. Prior to your interview sessions, you should prepare a sample contract if you have no current reps. If you already have a rep group, you'll have a basic contract for your new rep to review. It should spell out those company policies that are or will be consistent for all reps. Favoring one rep over another in contract terms will certainly cause problems, so stick to standard policies. Make certain that any changes will affect all reps. Commission rates, termination conditions, dates commissions are payable, and all other factors common to all your reps should be included in the sample contract.

Negotiable conditions, usually involving only the territory to be covered, are not included. These will be agreed upon during your final interview sessions and can be entered in ink at that time. Even if a rep agrees to its terms after a cursory review of your contract, it's wise to leave a copy with him. He may have overlooked a clause he doesn't understand or objects to. A contract in hand enables him to clear up any points of possible conflict before he receives the formal contract.

The territory to be covered by the rep will be the most protracted point of discussion, and since this can often decide the fate of negotiations, you should be ready to consider variations of the boundaries of your rep's territory.

Award the Territories Carefully

In the early days of the franchise business it was common to award licenses for large territories for a very small amount of money. This early naiveté came back to haunt the franchising companies, particularly the successful ones. Content with a good income, their franchisees ignored vast portions of their territory and they were powerless to exploit these areas because of the exclusive contract previously awarded. Their solution—a costly one—was to buy back the rights from the original franchisees and either open up company operations or divide the territories among many franchisees.

The company just starting its rep program can learn a lesson from the franchising companies' costly errors. It pays to award territories very carefully, thereby avoiding agonizing realignment efforts later. Too many novice sales managers think in terms of individual states or groups of states, rather than established marketing areas, which often include portions of a state.

MANA's marketing guide, on the following page, illustrates this point very well. New York City and its environs and part of New Jersey comprise one suggested marketing area and upstate New York another. Lower California is grouped with several Southwestern states, and the upper California area is allied with the state of Nevada. On the other hand, Florida, by itself, represents a separate territory for some manufacturers. MANA's guide is just that, a guide to your territorial division, and not a substitute for the careful analysis you must make of where and how your product is to be sold.

As you begin to develop a territorial marketing plan, it pays to retain as much flexibility as possible. This flexibility will help you in your negotiations with the reps you choose for your program. For instance, most manufacturers consider Texas and Oklahoma together as one marketing area. Reps based in either state usually serve the other. We've had to decline to represent some good firms that already have a rep in Kansas or Missouri who also covers Oklahoma. To work with these firms, we'd have to dilute our efforts whenever we called on an Oklahoma firm. I know of a good company that has been looking for a rep to cover Oklahoma and Arkansas for several years. A glance at MANA's guide will help you appreciate the difficulty of finding such a rep.

One of the keys to a successful division of territories will be the reps themselves. Older, more established rep firms will be more rigid in defining specific marketing areas. Through years of experience they've learned that their chosen area is most productive for their firm, and they're not interested in redesigning the area to accommodate a particular principal. A good example of this is this contract description of an area specified by a Pittsburgh rep firm for its principals.

> All of western Pennsylvania bordered on the east
> and including the counties of Tioga, Lycoming,
> Clinton, Centre, Mifflin, Huntingdon, and Franklin;
> also the bordering counties in New York consisting

MANA's MARKETING TERRITORIES

1. Eastern Massachusetts, Rhode Island, New Hampshire, Maine.
2. Connecticut, western Massachusetts, Vermont.
3. New York City, Long Island, Westchester County, New Jersey north of Trenton.
4. New York Upstate.
5. New Jersey, Trenton and south, Pennsylvania east of Harrisburg.
6. Maryland, Delaware, District of Columbia, northern Virginia.
7. Southern Virginia, North Carolina, South Carolina, eastern Tennessee.
8. Georgia and Alabama.
9. Florida.
10. Western Pennsylvania to Harrisburg, West Virginia.
11. Ohio north of Route 40.
12. Ohio south of Route 40, Kentucky.
13. Indiana except northwestern counties.
14. Michigan and Toledo, Ohio.
15. Illinois, north of Rt. 36 and Lake, Porter and LaPorte counties of Indiana.
16. Wisconsin and Northwestern Michigan (area northwest of Lake Michigan).
17. Minnesota. May include North and South Dakota and all or part of Iowa and Nebraska.
18. Eastern Missouri, southern Illinois.
19. Western Missouri, Kansas.
20. Louisiana, Mississippi, Arkansas, western Tennessee.
21. Texas and Oklahoma.
22. Colorado, Utah. May include Montana, Idaho, Wyoming.
23. California, Bakersfield and south, Arizona, Southern Nevada and New Mexico.
24. California, north of Bakersfield, part of Nevada.
25. Washington and Oregon.
26. Alaska.
27. Hawaii.
28. Puerto Rico.
29. Eastern Canada.
30. Western Canada.
31. International.

of Steuben, Allegany, Cattaraugus, and Chau-
tauqua.

All of West Virginia and the following bordering
counties in Ohio: Lawrence, Gallia, Meigs, Athens,
Washington, Monroe, Belmont, Jefferson, Colum-
biana, Mahoning, Trumbull, and Ashtabula.

This particular sample is somewhat extreme and could certainly cause
complications when territories in the neighboring states of New York
and Ohio are being negotiated, but it does give an indication of one
sales agency's interpretation of its most effective marketing area.

Although you'll have a designated territory in mind before interviewing candidates, you can benefit by listening to the reps describe
the areas they serve. If several good prospects are covering an area
slightly different from the one you envisioned, take a second look at
your outline. It may be that you've overlooked a combination of marketing territories better served by one rep firm than by two separate organizations.

Willingness to adjust your territory boundaries to the selling areas
defined by the natives can give you a leg up on a competitor with
inflexible marketing territories. *Business Control Atlas,* published by
American Map Company, may help you considerably in describing
your territories, particularly where counties are specified. This atlas
has individual maps of all the states and all the provinces of Canada.

Nonnegotiable Terms and Equal Treatment

Nonnegotiable terms of the contract include all clauses other than
those dealing with territorial assignments. The word nonnegotiable as
used here refers more to company policies than to a rigid set of conditions that can't be changed. As mentioned above, your company
should treat all reps equally; clauses covering the following policies
and conditions should therefore be the same in all your contracts:

Commissions on existing accounts
Exclusivity of territory
Commission rates and payment schedules
Commission policies on shipments into another territory
Noncompetitive lines

Responsibility and obligations of the rep
Responsibility and obligations of the principal
Hold harmless agreement
Term (length of contract) and conditions of termination
Sales policies
Travel expenses for sales meetings

Some companies include clauses in their contracts covering every conceivable condition that could arise; others are much simpler in their approach. Contracts usually reflect the philosophy of the company's owners or of a particularly influential law firm. Within reason, the simpler the contract the better. Some brief comments on a few of the standard clauses are given here to help you and your reps attain good working relationships.

Commissions on existing accounts. Theories abound on what the size of commissions should be on existing accounts within the rep's territory. Should you turn over all accounts at regular commissions or at reduced commissions? Should they be maintained as house accounts with no commission? Should commissions be paid on shipments made after the effective date of the contract or only on shipments of goods ordered after the contract becomes effective? And so on.

Because of the endless combinations of existing commission arrangements, let me give you a few simple guidelines on how the top companies pay commissions. After having chosen a rep, these companies expect the relationship to continue on a long-term basis, much as they would on hiring a direct employee. A new direct employee is enrolled in the company insurance plan and is given all other fringe benefits the company offers. He's not "on trial," but is welcomed and made to feel he's part of the company.

A new rep firm is welcomed with the same enthusiasm. All existing business is turned over to it at normal contract rates. One of my firms paid us commissions on shipments made immediately after the contract was signed, though the orders had been entered prior to the signing of the contract. In this case the firm had no previous rep in the area, and thus no one was entitled to these commissions. Nevertheless it was a magnanimous gesture, and our enthusiasm and incentive for a company that operates in such a fair manner are boundless.

Simply put, the more professional you are in your commission payments, the better the rep you'll be able to hire. House accounts, reduced commissions, or delayed commissions don't represent an all-out commitment to the rep, and sensing a lack of professionalism on this score, he in turn will find it hard to make an all-out commitment to your firm.

Exclusivity of territory. All business received from the awarded area should be credited to the rep firm serving that area. Without an "exclusive" for his territory, your rep will probably never achieve the sales you expect from him. He can't freely solicit business for your company if you make him constantly prove that orders coming from his customers were indeed initiated by his efforts. In such an unfavorable situation he may concentrate on a few regular customers to the exclusion of other attractive accounts. Furthermore, most reputable reps insist upon exclusivity. If you insist on a nonexclusive contract you'll find the ranks of your prospective reps thinned to an alarming degree.

With an exclusive agreement, your rep will use all his talents and energy to bring you increased sales. One of our principals recently received a nice order direct from a company whose project engineer had visited our booth at a local trade show over a year and a half earlier. He had talked to us about our products and took along our descriptive literature. Now, long after we had forgotten his visit, he was ready to buy our company's product—and we, of course, received a commission. Without the protection afforded us by an "exclusive," we wouldn't have had the incentive to invest time and money in promotional events such as trade shows where results may not be apparent for months.

We now publish an informative newsletter featuring case studies and other helpful data about the products of our principals. We press these on anyone who remotely resembles a potential customer, and inquiries and orders are often received directly by our companies as a result of this widespread distribution. Again, we can't tie down every order resulting from this newsletter, so without an exclusive arrangement, no newsletter would be published.

Commission rates and payment schedules. A simple rule to follow in setting commission rates is to examine the existing rate structure of your industry and stay as close as possible to the norm. A rate higher than that can mean noncompetitive pricing for your products; a lower rate will fail to attract the quality of rep you're seeking.

As a matter of interest only, an AMA survey of average commis-

MANUFACTURERS' REPRESENTATIVES' COMMISSIONS

| | | Range of Commissions | |
Industry	Average Commission	Low	High
Consumer Products			
Consumer-Durable	5.0%	1.0%	15.0%
Food Products	4.5	3.0	5.0
Major Household Items	5.8	—	—
Proprietary Drugs and Toiletries	5.0	—	—
Industrial Products			
Aerospace Products	7.5	2.0	15.0
Automotive Parts and Accessories	5.0	2.0	10.0
Building Materials	6.0	4.0	10.0
Electrical	7.0	5.0	11.0
Electronics	7.0	3.0	20.0
Fabrics	5.0	—	—
Instruments	15.0	4.0	27.0
Iron and Steel	5.0	1.5	15.0
Machinery (Light and Heavy)	15.0	3.0	40.0
Metal Products (Light and Heavy)	7.5	1.3	30.0
Paper	5.0	—	—
Rubber, Plastics and Leather	4.0	3.0	10.0
Tools and Hardware	5.0	—	—

Source: AMA Executive Compensation Service *Sales Personnel* Report, 20th Edition, 1975.

sion rates paid to reps in a variety of industries is shown in the accompanying table. This is not to be used as a guide, since averages tend to mislead, but it'll give you some insight into the ranges of rates that can apply in any one industry.

To obtain a particularly attractive piece of business you'll sometimes have to minimize profit margins, and it'll be tempting to ask the rep to join in the sacrifice. Most top firms choose to avoid this sticky matter, and either go after the business based on the full commission rate or forget the order. Although it's best to be consistent about such a policy, many firms do include a clause in the contract that gives them the right to adjust commissions either with or without agreement on the part of the rep. If your company has such a clause, it's best to allow for consultation with and approval by the rep prior to entering an order based on paying a reduced commission.

When as sales manager I was occasionally confronted by this dilemma, I'd work very closely with the rep concerned. We usually agreed to a production cost analysis on a new part we were after. I'd analyze our costs on production runs to determine if our minimum profit structure could be realized, and the rep would agree to a reduced commission. Knowing that estimators tend to exaggerate costs when quoting a part in order to be fully protected, we'd agree to raise the rep's commission commensurate with the increase in profit that we'd usually realize after one or two production runs. This worked to everyone's satisfaction but necessitated the rep's complete trust in our honesty. I recommend against such a procedure on a routine basis because of suspicions that can be aroused if the hoped-for increase in commission is not forthcoming.

Timing of commission payments is an important feature of your contract. In surveying reps on this question I found that almost 60 percent received their commissions in the month following shipment. This, of course, is an ideal arrangement. Your reps may have spent months or even years trying to nail down a new account. They've incurred expenditures well in advance of the ultimate shipping date, and to keep them waiting until you've been paid is unfair. You and your firm's employees are paid on a regular basis regardless of when goods are shipped; the rep should be extended the same courtesy.

Naturally a new firm is often confronted by a shortage of working capital and seeks to minimize cash outflow. Paying reps after the company has been paid improves the cash flow situation, and many small companies need to begin in this fashion. Once cash flow is satisfactory, however, you'll find that sending out commissions the month after shipment will increase your standing with the reps and reduce your own and your rep's paperwork by a considerable amount.

Delaying payment of commissions beyond contractual agreements is to be avoided at all costs. This clouds the relationship between you and your reps. They're being asked to bear a portion of the cost of your inability to run your business efficiently. Extended use of this device to regulate cash flow will end the association. It may also result in a lawsuit that will prove costly for both parties. Prompt payments of agreed-upon commissions are essential to a good continuing relationship with your rep firms.

Commission policies on shipment into another territory. When an order originates in one rep's territory but is shipped into another's, commissions are usually paid to the former rep, but exceptions are made. If the product requires servicing by the rep into whose territory it's shipped, or demonstrations are required at the customer's plant, but the order is placed by a centralized purchasing department in another state, then the latter may receive payment. There are endless variations on this theme, and based on your product and how it's sold and serviced, you'll have to determine how you're going to allocate commissions when these circumstances of multiple selling and servicing arise.

The importance of consistency can't be overemphasized. After the necessary trial-and-error period, readjust your policies and be sure they apply to all reps fairly.

Noncompetitive lines. When interviewing a rep you'll review his principals to ascertain that their lines don't represent competition to your company's product. If you're satisfied that they don't, you shouldn't subsequently demand that your rep stop carrying them—unless you've been the victim of misleading information or product lines are changed and expanded. However, you should reserve the right to approve the rep's acceptance of future lines that could infringe on his sale of your product. A good rep will consult with you prior to entering serious negotiations with a firm that even remotely appears to be a competitor. It's then your obligation to make a thorough investigation of that company's product and deliver a prompt decision.

In your analysis, remember that a product similar to yours but indirectly, or only slightly, competitive can increase your own sales by providing a wider range of potential customers for your rep, and thus for you. We've been turned down by principals in two or three instances where we presented them with companies we thought would be excellent counterparts to their product lines. In each instance, however, they were thorough in their analysis and we accepted their decisions without prejudice, though we felt that an opportunity had been missed.

Responsibility and obligations of the rep. It's good practice to set out working guidelines for your reps. Naturally, they should be expected to do their best to sell your products, and this responsibility should be spelled out in the contract. Because of the unique arrangement wherein the rep and the company seek as close a working relationship as possible and yet are not personally responsible for each other's actions, it's important that the contract definitely set out the legal limits of the rep's authority.

In conformance with common legal practice, it should be plainly stated that while the rep may solicit business for the firm he may not accept orders from or make commitments to a customer without express authorization from the company he represents. In other words, as an independent contractor he's responsible for the actions of his own firm, but he provides only a service to his principal. The rep can forward a price to a customer but does not have the right to negotiate or change the price without the company's authorization. He can't authorize the return of rejected goods. He can't approve the credit of a customer. All these decisions and the authority they represent are the responsibility of the principal.

Some companies ask reps for aid in collecting sums owed them by customers. While outside the realm of a rep's regular duties, this assistance is expected in the case of a poor credit risk. Since the rep has no authority to set credit terms, it's inconsistent to expect him to attempt collections when the principal's credit department has erred in assessing a customer's ability to pay on time. More important, pursuit of overdue funds introduces a negative selling note: a rep should not approach his customer in the role of a collection agent. Nevertheless, a company habitually in arrears on bills and in danger of default is normally not a good long-term business prospect. My agency will usually attempt to recover funds due from this type of company.

A company in poor condition should not be confused with well-financed organizations whose normal practice is to delay payment of bills for a predetermined number of months so they can use their cash for a longer period. This type of firm will tell you bluntly that you'll have to wait for your money if you want their business. This is a matter for your company's credit department to resolve; a rep's constant request for payment can only annoy the purchasing people whose goodwill he relies on for continued business.

Responsibility and obligations of the principal. Your commitment to your reps is also important, and here you have an opportunity to make positive statements about your obligations that contrast favorably with the legalistic jargon so common in the average contract.

Why not work on this clause with a little extra vigor and enthusiasm? Tell the rep, in your own style, that your company is dedicated to selling through manufacturers' representatives. Subtly back up that statement with a description of what you're going to do for *him*. You'll provide a consistent advertising program; you'll keep him supplied with current literature; you'll send him all sales leads promptly; you'll make regular trips into the field; you'll do your best to quote competitive prices and maintain delivery promises; and maybe you'll even accept a certain quota of collect calls.

Under this clause the rep is used to seeing some perfunctory phrase that outlines minimum company obligations. If you surprise him with a sincere and generous statement in the contract itself, you'll provide a stimulus that'll get him started with enthusiasm. However, don't include promises here that you don't intend to keep. Hollow promises do more harm than good.

Hold harmless agreement. Product liability has taken on a new connotation in the past few years with the explosive development of consumer consciousness. The new era of government-sponsored consumer attacks on the manufacturing community has caused many headaches—some deservedly so—for all companies, whatever their product. It has also created one new headache for your rep: the possibility of expensive legal fees should he and your company be included in a lawsuit over defective merchandise manufactured by your company. Fortunately, you have a relatively low-cost remedy available to help him: product liability insurance. By including the rep in your coverage and including a "hold harmless" clause in your contract, you may save him from expensive legal costs.

Attorneys suing a company for damages because some real or imagined shortcoming in its product has harmed their client tend to include in their charges anyone within shouting distance of the product. This usually includes your rep, if he was involved in the sale of the product. The fact that judges have been releasing reps from most litigation involving product liability in no way frees the rep from having to spend a considerable amount of money in legal fees. Despite precedents, your rep's attorney must make a thorough investigation of the facts, and these data-gathering costs can be extensive. A hold harmless clause in your contract that protects the rep and includes his legal costs as part of your obligation should not be expensive for your firm and will be a welcome addition to your contract.

Term (length of contract) and conditions of termination. Bluntly stated, the length of the contract and the conditions for termination have long been the greatest source of controversy in principal-rep relationships. Principals feel they should have the right to terminate a rep pretty much at will—just as they have with an employee—for financial or any other reasons deemed in the interest of the profitable conduct of their business. Reps feel they're different from employees in that they expend their own funds and time in soliciting business for their principals and should therefore be entitled to a substantial grace period to recoup these expenses when termination occurs.

The heart of the controversy is not the right to terminate but the conditions that accompany such action. In its short-form agency agreement, MANA suggests that a 120-day notice be given in the event of termination after a minimum of one year's association. In addition, the rep should receive commissions on all orders solicited (but not necessarily placed) prior to the termination date. At the other end of the line, some companies employ a 30-day termination notice, with the rep entitled to commissions on goods shipped only within that 30-day period, regardless of the dollar volume of orders received prior to the termination date.

I think the fair solution is somewhere between these two extremes, with longevity of the principal-rep association dictating the conditions of termination. For example, some enlightened companies seeking to be fair to both parties will start with a 30-day termination condition and add 30 days to this for each year the relationship has been in effect, extending to a maximum of 120 to 360 days. These conditions give proof of the company's desire for a successful long-term association with its reps and also afford the reps a certain amount of protection against a future management that may decide to eliminate the rep program.

No contract, of course, protects a rep against the unscrupulous company that concludes an agreement for the purpose of gaining a cheap entry into a marketplace with the intent to switch from reps to company salesmen once volume reaches an attractive level. Another ploy—practiced by a fastener firm in my territory—was to change reps completely once a year, thus gaining a new group of customers with each new rep. This is a short-sighted policy, since word traveled quickly in rep circles once the company's strategy was exposed. Their success at attracting new reps has gone from bad to worse ever since.

Recently Congress has gotten into the act because of the practices of a minority of firms that attempted to trade on the sales rep's goodwill. *Sales Management* magazine (March 17, 1975) reported that Representative John Y. McCollister (R.–Neb.) introduced a bill stipulating that a rep who had been terminated through no fault of his own receive payment of 0.5 percent of the gross sales he realized in his area. This payment would be due on business received after termination for a period equal to the length of time he had been under contract to the manufacturer. If he had been associated with the principal for over five years, the compensation rate would be one percent. To protect manufacturers from unscrupulous reps, payment would be due only on business developed initially by the rep and serviced for a minimum of 18 months prior to cancellation.

This bit of legislation, which at first glance appears to favor the rep, can perhaps prevent him from taking on a more profitable competing line for several years, while at the same time it reduces his commissions (1 percent to 0.5 percent) from previous principals. However, it's an interesting effort to afford more protection to rep firms in their termination conditions. Fortunately, veteran companies accustomed to working with reps bend over backward to avoid termination action, seeking rather to help the rep reach the mutual goals that will bring them both the profit that is the purpose of the association.

When you write the termination clause of your contract, give it a good deal of thought and place yourself in your rep's shoes. Keep in mind that you'll be working with your reps over a long period of time. You wouldn't want to see a fellow employee thrown out into the cold overnight; you should also not want to be the cause of a similar harmful act to a rep. Remember, your company can be sold or transferred to a new management within a short period of time, and the subsequent management team may have an entirely different philosophy from yours about the sales program and its implementation, possibly resulting in wholesale sacking of your faithful rep force. By drawing up a fair termination clause, you'll have performed a service to your reps and your company.

Getting the Rep to Sign

The good offices of MANA are always available to assist your company and your attorney. Over the years this body has come to grips with the realities of contract contents, good and bad, and has developed both a short- and a long-form sample contract outlining most of the accepted practices in the rep industry. These are offered free to members and can be purchased by nonmembers for $10 each.

In the last few years, prodded by the government, the insurance industry has greatly simplified the language of its insurance forms so that the layman can understand his coverage more fully. This commendable practice should be followed in your contracts, and if you have a particularly progressive lawyer you can perhaps set your own landmarks in simplifying rep contract forms by eliminating some whereins and wherefores and coming up with a truly understandable contract.

If you develop a contract that's equitable to both parties, you'll have little trouble getting a good rep's signature on the dotted line, and you can then quickly get on to the more productive aspect of your relationship: bringing in the orders.

Part Two

MOTIVATING
THE PROFESSIONALS

8

COMMUNICATION

No communication, no sale

A successful rep program begins with the hiring of a competent group of professional commissioned sales representatives, but regardless of the caliber of its personnel, a rep program left to its own devices will soon falter. With good, strongly motivated leadership, however, results can be startlingly productive and should be financially highly rewarding to your company.

Part Two of this book is designed to make you aware of the many motivational practices required to keep a rep force working effectively. You'll also learn a variety of simple and elaborate supplemental strategies that can make the difference between a good rep sales program and a great one.

The Rep Has to Know

This chapter deals specifically with communication, but succeeding chapters will demonstrate that all motivating actions are vitally involved with communication. The success of sales meetings, advertising programs, and technical assistance is in every instance determined by successful communication, and your skill and imagination in developing a continuing and consistent program will be reflected in the sales results you obtain.

Unfortunately, the word "communication" has become a catchall in industry today, encompassing both the good and the bad. Fads in communication are omnipresent. Untold millions of dollars are spent, mostly by the larger corporations, developing the most effective means of keeping harmony in the ranks and providing employees with meaningful interpretations of their jobs.

Behaviorial scientists have entered the market with a gusto unmatched since time study was invented. I've participated in more "Theory Y" seminars than I care to remember and several others in which the ability to communicate was a strong factor in the success of the theory. Undoubtedly, some of the theories have strengthened company interpersonal relationships, but the cost for these scattered successes has been enormous.

Perhaps the very word "theory" describes the difficulty inherent in submitting business processes to a procedure that appears logical but has not been tested under the pressurized demands of industry where instant action is often required. For instance, it's hard to convince a production manager whose $3-million production line is shut down for lack of a particular component that he should call a meeting and let a committee probe the whys and wherefores of getting the line started—even though he's been told this conforms with some of the more daring philosophies of the behaviorial scientists.

Of course there are less sophisticated psychological stratagems that we all use from time to time to deal with our everyday problems, and this is the path that I recommend the sales manager follow in his working relationships with his reps. Be flexible but simple—not because reps won't respond to sophisticated communication, but because they're action-motivated men and they prefer not to wade through a lot of gingerbread to get at the substance of your message. Psychological niceties are wasted on them: the more directly you deal with them, the quicker they'll respond.

As company executives, you and your associates are in contact with the day-to-day changes in your operation. When the supply of raw materials becomes critical, or a flu epidemic hits your production people, or a gas shortage threatens to reduce your workweek, you know it, and you automatically adjust your delivery promises on quotations. But unaware of these internal problems, your reps blithely continue to promise shipment of your goods in 10 weeks instead of the 16 weeks it'll take under the new set of production circumstances.

Often, only after a customer calls to complain about late delivery on his new order does the rep realize that lead times have lengthened.

This embarrassing and potentially harmful situation can easily be avoided by sending a simple bulletin to reps indicating any substantial change in lead times. One of our principals in Cleveland, a short-run metal-stamping house, thoughtfully informs us in this manner whenever lead times change, greatly increasing our ability to serve our customers. It knows that we know what's going on. This is one example of a supplemental service that requires little expense and time but increases thhe credibility of your rep with his customers.

Purchasing people who object to reps—and a considerable number do—see the rep as too much of a generalist, not sufficiently up to date with his principals' practices and policies. Too often they're right. However, the fault usually lies with a principal's lack of concern about keeping its reps fully informed. No rep can be more effective than you allow him to be. The more information you give him about anything and everything, the better able he'll be to represent you in the field.

What the Rep Has to Know

This brings us to several essentials of communication that are the minimum you can afford to provide and still expect encouraging returns on your investment in your rep program.

Quotations. This is the one area in which most companies do well. We receive copies of all quotes made by our principals. It isn't too difficult—an extra carbon in the typewriter is all it takes—and in my view the majority of reps can't fault their principals for lack of attention to this detail. But of course there's room for improvement.

Many firms are exceedingly skimpy about details. As a sales manager I received numerous requests from our more progressive reps that copies of blueprints be sent along with our quotes, specifying exceptions we had taken to our customers' design. For the life of me—I was much younger then—I couldn't see why they needed this type of information. Ultimately, with the help of a patient and experienced rep who backed up his request with a recitation of a sequence of events leading to a lost order, I was able to see the light.

A customer who had received our competitive quote had questioned my rep about our objection to a minor tolerance. This purchasing agent was particularly uncooperative, and when my rep professed ignorance of the blueprint details, the order, an attractive piece of business, was awarded to a competitor. After that incident, all our reps received a copy of the marked-up print with every quote. Ironically, our tolerance deviation could easily have been resolved in this case and we lost an order that should have been ours.

Many orders are lost because of the omission of seemingly unimportant details that are vital to a buyer's appraisal of a quotation. Are all specifications met? Will the product be packaged as requested? Is the delivery firm? Is the price firm? Often buyers will place an order with a company that answers all aspects of the inquiry, even though its price may be higher, rather than go back to the lower bidders and ask for a clarification of omitted details.

Order acknowledgments. Here, too, most companies are consistent in their practice of sending reps copies of acknowledgments, although somewhat less so than in mailing copies of quotations.

More progressive companies have devised a multiple-use form. The original is sent to the customer; this gives him all the information he needs to insure that the principal has correctly entered the order—quantity, product description, price, time of delivery, and any possible exceptions that may be taken to the customer's requirements or demands are included on this original. The remaining copies, one of which is mailed to the rep, have all the above information, but may include additional data meant to expedite the internal processing of the order but of no interest to the customer. These details perhaps identify the piece of equipment the product will be made on, specify the expected delivery date of the raw material, or even give instructions covering part of the product processing to be done by an outside source.

A copy of this detailed form can be very helpful to the rep because, being privy to much of the order's processing details, he can answer a buyer's questions more intelligently. To illustrate, a company making a unit from a raw material that's in short supply or that must be imported can run into procurement difficulties. By virtue of his awareness of the nature of the raw material and its probable source, a rep can mollify a buyer by explaining the delay in delivery without having to annoy plant personnel with numerous calls or letters.

Naturally, any information passed on to the rep in the order acknowledgment must be used judiciously. A source of supply of a scarce raw material skillfully discovered by your purchasing department could be turned into a disadvantage if a customer finds out about it. He could pass this information along to one of your competitors in an effort to obtain a more favorable price. A discerning rep will know what information to keep confidential, however, and the overall bene-fit of keeping him fully informed about an order should outweigh any possible risks.

Through receiving a copy of your acknowledgment, a rep can also avoid embarrassing incidents that might reduce his importance in the eyes of the customer. One of my regular sales trips covers over 1,000 miles, which means I can make this circuit only once every two or three months. On too many occasions I've failed to thank a customer for a fine order sent directly to the principal because I never received an acknowledgment copy of the order. I've thus missed many opportu-nities to register a favorable impression on a customer I see only on widely separated visits.

That same customer may ask about the delivery status of a particu-lar order, and again I'm at a loss to provide the information. My effec-tiveness with him is limited because he senses that I can't be of much help, and sooner or later a rep whose company keeps him up to date on order information can walk away with the account. This happened to us with a good customer, which upset our principal no end. If the principal had understood the role its reps play in all phases of finding, selling, and servicing customers, this disagreeable situation would have been avoided.

Finally, order acknowledgments allow a rep to run his business ef-ficiently. He must keep records of his backlog and be able to check shipments and invoices against commission payments. By not giving him copies of order acknowledgments you deprive him of the ability to keep accurate financial records. In short, give your rep all the informa-tion you can on your order acknowledgment form—he'll use it to your best advantage.

Order revisions. For the same reason that reps should receive cop-ies of order acknowledgments, they should receive notification of any changes affecting an order: increases or decreases in quantity or price, revisions in delivery, changes in design, and, of course, cancellations.

Shipping notices and invoices. If your company sends a shipping notice at time of shipment and mails invoices several days or weeks later, it's essential that a rep receive copies of both. If you mail in-voices almost immediately after shipment, then a copy of the invoice will suffice. Either document tells the rep that the product has been shipped. With this notification in hand, he can call an anxious buyer who, because of possible delays in receiving his copy of the invoice, will be happy to know his order is on the way.

Also, of course, your rep is interested in the amount of the invoice and the commission that will result. He looks forward to his payday as much as you do. And again the information helps him keep good financial records.

Correspondence with the customer. Since reps spend more time in the field than in their office, a good deal of correspondence involving all aspects of the business relationship takes place directly between the principal and the customer. It's essential that a rep receive copies of his principals' letters that concern him.

But receiving a copy of your reply to a customer without receiving a copy of the customer's correspondence is like listening to one end of a phone conversation—it leaves much to the imagination. An unimportant change in shipping instructions or a similar minor deviation is of course no cause for a flood of copies, but any correspondence of relative importance to the status of an order, or to a customer's concern or complaint, should be passed along to the rep.

If correspondence involves a serious complaint, it's essential that the rep be informed, lest he walk into a customer's office unarmed with advance knowledge of a possible confrontation. His awareness of the problem at hand and his clear understanding of his principal's stand can prevent a bad situation from getting worse. He can then gauge the seriousness and depth of the customer's dissatisfaction and help his principal decide on a course of action.

Occasionally a conflict of personalities arises between a purchasing man and certain personnel at the principal's company. Although unwilling to relay his feelings to the principal, the purchasing man may confide in the local rep. By explaining this conflict to the sales manager, a rep can help bring about a change in the personnel handling this specific customer, and the loss of a good customer can be prevented.

A consistent flow of copies of significant correspondence also helps the rep to understand your company's policies and philosophy and makes him a better representative. Knowing how to field penetrating questions about cancellation charges, technical assistance to be provided, and a host of other policy matters gives him a better credibility rating whenever he solicits business from a potential customer. This is doubly important in the months immediately following his coming on board with your organization. During this "basic training," he'll be unsure of your reactions to the expectations of certain customers; he'll tread carefully and—unfortunately—hesitantly, thus precluding the bold and confident approach so necessary to effective selling.

Shortly after we signed with one of our principals, he lent us his complete files on customers in our area. By reading through this correspondence, we were able to begin selling immediately with great confidence, secure in the knowledge that our declarations of that company's policies were accurate. We were saved both from being timid in our selling efforts and from making the usual number of mistakes while developing a sure conception of our client's policies. I'd encourage this method of company orientation both as a time- and money-saving device and as a quick stimulus to a rep's forceful entry into the field on your behalf.

Another of our companies gives us a copy of many of its internal memos. These can range from information about new hirings within their engineering department to a statement about a new emphasis on telephone manners when talking to customers. Each trivial or important bit makes us feel more a part of the organization, and we in turn have more confidence in selling its product. Normally, no one thinks of telling reps of the company's internal changes, some of which can give that company a tremendous advantage in a rep's territory because of a specialty requirement in a customer's plant that only the rep was aware of. If we're informed of a new piece of equipment that will make a certain type of part quicker and cheaper, for example, we can go back after business we had to pass up in the past.

How the Rep Gets to Know

You can't err by giving a rep too much information, and often one little piece of information, apparently of no consequence, can provide the spark that will ignite a whole new business relationship. Two opportunities for communication that must not be missed are provided by the postal service and the telephone company.

Correspondence with the rep. When a rep takes the time to write you and ask a question, answer him. Salesmen, direct and self-employed, aren't famous for their letter writing. The letters or notes they do write are short and to the point. If you have a rep who'll take the time to jot off a note from the field or work late in the office to complete his correspondence, you've got a gem; don't discourage him. The first thing you can do to keep him writing is to answer him by return mail; and if his request is relatively urgent, pick up the phone and call him.

One of the chief obstacles to prompt replies to rep correspondence is the time you spend out of the office. Letters can lay on the desk unanswered for a week or more simply because of your absence. There are several ways around this roadblock. (1) In your daily phone call to the office, ask your secretary to brief you on the more important correspondence and dictate a short reply to the immediate questions, with a follow-up letter on your return. (2) Delegate the letter-answering duty to a sales correspondent. A reply needing your authorization or O.K. can be handled over the phone between you and your sales correspondent. Often an experienced secretary can be an effective sales correspondent. (3) Use the phone to reply.

A prompt reply of some kind to a rep's letter is mandatory, or you'll find his enthusiasm tailing off quickly. A friend of mine who represents an excellent company in the heavier-component field not only doesn't receive prompt replies to his letters but doesn't receive any reply at all. If he phones the company at his own expense, he may or may not receive a reliable answer to his question, and promises to call him back with the requested information are seldom honored. Ironically, this company makes a first-rate product; my friend says he could double its business in his territory if it would improve its communications.

Phone calls. The phone is the handiest piece of equipment to come along since the wheel, at least as far as progressive companies and their reps are concerned. But few companies and reps use it to best advantage.

I regularly receive phone calls from a West Coast principal around six in the evening at home. The sales manager is back from his day's outing and is current on any outstanding matters we have hanging fire. Knowing I enjoy a precooled predinner martini, he seems to time his calls so that after our discussion I can relax with my drink, which is inevitably placed in the freezer just before his call. We can clear up a great deal of current business with these short business phone calls.

If it's urgent that you reach a rep on the road, evening is always the best time to phone him. It's a rare rep who doesn't leave his itinerary and motel locations with his wife, so you can bank on her knowing how to reach him if he's not at home.

I'd guess that cost is one of the major influences against business use of this communication marvel to its fullest advantage. However, a little attention to the special arrangements available will apprise you of the significant savings possible through a combination of the correct equipment and the judicious timing of your calls.

The place to begin your investigation is not with the telephone companies, although I bear no grudge toward them. Like any other sales-oriented firm, their managements want the highest return possible on their investments of money and effort, and while I doubt that they'd try to recommend a lot of equipment you don't need, they're certainly not anxious to prescribe the minimum necessary facilities.

Some consultant firms employ ex-phone-company personnel who are experts in recommending economical equipment and practices. They can save you much expense and increase your effective use of the telephone. If your company is big enough, you'll be charged a percentage of the first year's savings; if it's smaller, you may be quoted a fee. Either way, you seldom lose.

What we're after, however, is more use of the phone to increase your sales. A call to a harried purchasing agent in immediate need of a product can bring an order—perhaps even at a higher price than a competitor's if the competitor can't submit his bid as fast as you can. By supplying a rep with a lead on a new company in the area he'll be visiting during his upcoming extensive business trip, your call can bring about a prompt visit and a new customer if your rep is there first with a needed product.

The list of the advantages you can realize by proper use of the phone is endless, so if your management is parsimonious about long-distance calls, get started soon on checking out alternatives to your present telephone policies.

The Ideal Communicator: Two Examples

It's an unusual individual who has the courage to admit his mistakes, but such candor about oneself usually implies another quality—the ability to profit from one's errors. Such a person is Oren Northcutt, president of Dal-Air Tool Co. in Point, Texas, who frankly confided to me that his lack of knowledge about communication was the primary reason for his losing a complete sales force of fourteen reps.

Oren invented and markets a unique air tool for automotive mechanics. His practice was to hire a rep, send him a few brochures, and wait for the orders to arrive. Strangely enough, some orders did arrive; Oren attributes this fortunate turn of events to the one or two self-starters in his rep force who sold his air tool despite the total lack of communication or field support from Dal-Air. The balance of his group—good, workmanlike reps, but typical sales people—turned their attention to the products of other principals, who motivated them through constant attention to their communication needs: prompt quotes, quick answers to their queries, and occasional field trips.

Because of a successful change in marketing strategy, Oren is not following the rep route today in his air-tool sales. Rather, in keeping with his entrepreneurial instincts, he started a small foundry a few years back at a time of high industrial activity when his investment casting suppliers could not or would not furnish him castings for his air tools. Later, when several of these castings were replaced in his production by more economical components, he decided to solicit business for his foundry from outside sources. Sales in the casting business are inevitably made through reps, and having learned from his past experiences, Oren is proceeding with an intelligent, progressive rep policy that has already brought a heartening increase in business.

At present four firms represent him. These were carefully chosen, one at a time, as Dal-Air's facilities were increased to handle a larger volume. New reps will be added only when Oren's foundry capacity is again increased, thus enabling it to absorb a larger sales volume without disturbing its ability to provide current customers with the good, dependable service they count on.

Oren seldom takes more than a week to give a quote on a part—a real plus for the rep who often loses an order because of delayed quotes. He replies promptly to correspondence from his reps and encourages them to visit his plant to gain a better understanding of the capabilities of the investment casting process. An initial brochure limits itself to illustrating the range of his facilities, but more sophisticated literature is being planned. There's no doubt in my mind that this time around Oren will wind up with a highly productive sales program that will be financially rewarding to both him and his sales reps—and all because of his frank recognition of his previous unintentional neglect of his rep group's communication needs.

Let me finish with an account of another firm that in my opinion has developed as fine a rep program as will be found anywhere in industry. Arrow Gear Company of Downers Grove, Illinois, is the leading quality manufacturer of spiral bevel gears in the country. (I'm prejudiced, of course.) Because of its expertise in right-angle gearing, the company is widely known and receives a good amount of business. But rather than rest on its laurels and accept business that comes its way through its reputation, it conducts a rep sales program that's a joy to behold.

Again, "communication" is the core of its success. As soon as an inquiry is received from a company in my area, a copy of that inquiry is sent to me, thus alerting me to significant activity at a local firm. This knowledge allows me to plan my next itinerary in anticipation of a likely sale.

A prompt quotation is then mailed—or phoned, if necessary—together with a delivery promise. The general manager does most of the quoting; if he's away on business, the president pitches in and gets the quotes out—or, in the president's absence, the sales correspondent sees that the job gets done. The sales correspondent is in the office 100 percent of the time and so has all order details at his fingertips; when I make a long-distance call for information, his rapid responses save us money.

The sales manager and the general manager make regular trips to our area, and because of their expertise they frequently spot opportunities we may have missed while touring customers' plants. At my own end, when a customer has a design question, I can pick up the phone in his office and contact the general manager or chief engineer, both of whom are ready and willing to offer assistance in solving the customer's problem.

We receive a monthly memo on new accounts developed by the reps and frequent communications about anything that will help us sell the company's gears. Sales leads are sent at least monthly and offer numerous opportunities for new business. Commissions are paid promptly the month following the invoice date. No fancy quotas are assigned; the company simply requests a yearly forecast of what we think will come out of the area.

There are other striking uses of communication that Arrow utilizes, but these are proprietary and must remain unmentioned to protect the company's competitive advantage in its industry.

Fortunately, we have other principals that follow closely behind Arrow in their objective to provide us with maximum support. They see that their reps are given every possible competitive break in their efforts to bring in business. When we visited his plant, one sales supervisor told us, "We want you to think of our company as No. 1 among your principals in supporting your efforts in the field." He obviously meant it—and his company's dedicated efforts strongly back up his avowed intentions.

Many companies are missing good rep results because they don't realize that they must compete with other companies for the reps' selling time. Your strongest competitors, in most instances, are those companies among his principals that religiously follow the doctrine of consistent, productive communication with their sales reps. The more he knows when he sits in front of Mr. Purchasing Agent, the more confidently your rep can perform his function of selling your product.

9

COMPETITIVE PRICING, TOP QUALITY, AND EXCELLENT SERVICE

Keys to a productive rep program

Good communication is essential, but it can't take the place of a well-rounded support program. Your product must be needed, must be well made and dependable, must be priced at a level consistent with your industry's pricing structure, and must be delivered on time. Only then will you reap the benefits of a good communications effort.

We once worked for a firm that inundated us with data. We received monthly computer forms outlining every conceivable detail of a customer's order: price, delivery date promised, shipments made, nomenclature of each part involved, and value of all orders on the books. This last piece of information ultimately became of little interest because the company, awash in a sea of paperwork, forgot that other support functions were also necessary to maintaining a good flow of business.

Actually, this firm was not naive about its shortcomings. I surmise from their actions that the top managers decided to make all the money they could during a high-demand period, and purposely ignored their customer service obligations to achieve their short-sighted goal.

When business activity slowed to a more regular pace, this firm instructed its reps to return to former customers, hat in hand, and drum up business by promising greater attention to important details in the future. This is a difficult and often futile task for a rep. True, during times of high demand all companies suffer some inadequacies in servicing their customers, but if a serious attempt is made to keep promised commitments, customers will understand and stay with a conscientious supplier. However, when it becomes apparent that a company has adopted a philosophy of taking advantage of overdemand to reap a large profit at the customers' expense, no amount of apologies or promises will bring back lost business—which is exactly what happened to this company.

Keep the Price Competitive

If reps have heard one statement from prospective principals more than any other, it is: "We may not have the lowest prices in the industry, but we develop a good rapport with customers and provide them with a quality product." This is usually uttered by a sales manager with no current business in the area, and generates a sinking feeling in the pit of the rep's stomach, especially when it comes at the end of what was a pretty successful interview.

The statement in itself is not suspect; we represent several firms whose prices are not the lowest, but who are highly successful because they give their customers excellent quality and service. Too often, though, the statement is an excuse for the company's inability or lack of intent to price its product competitively in a rep's area. There may be several reasons for noncompetitive pricing, but a good rep will not take on the firm unless the company has proved its statement is valid through prior successful selling in the area.

When you have little or no business in an area, you should do some homework to ascertain whether you can compete pricewise in the territory you're attempting to penetrate. If few companies in that area are making a competitive product, you may find a market that will allow a good profit margin on your regular pricing structure. On the other hand, if many firms are competing with your product, corners may have to be cut on your profit margin.

One of the best gauges of the competitive climate is the number and quality of replies you receive to your advertisements for reps. If the replies are few or of poor quality, that can mean the market is already saturated with your product and price competition is so severe that knowledgeable reps are concentrating their efforts on products offering more sales potential. If in doubt about spending money on a rep search program, seek out reps handling similar lines or make a personal comprehensive survey of potential customers.

If you find the market promising and decide to enter it, make certain that your prices are competitive. If possible, they should be lower than the competition's, to gain the attention of purchasing agents and buyers who have never heard of you. Even though your rep may have an established relationship with a buyer, a good price will give his attempt to introduce your product a better chance of success.

A rep's continued attention to the sale of your company's products depends on their pricing stability. An artificially inflated initial price followed by numerous bargaining sessions—each lowering the price a bit more—is time-wasting and expensive for the rep. He wants to follow up a quote, see where he stands, and enter into final negotiations for the order. You may ask, "Who doesn't?" But numerous companies seem compelled to go through the entire give-and-take charade for each order. The few orders they receive at an inflated price aren't worth the time consumed by these antics on each and every quote. A good rep simply can't afford to spend the time this procedure demands.

A competitive price with a fair profit structure is all we ask. Naturally, larger orders normally require negotiations before they're placed. Such discussions may involve factors other than price that usually affect in-plant costs—for example, spread-out deliveries at the quoted price, or holding the product to a particularly critical tolerance. But this type of negotiation is expected by the rep, since both the firm and the customer must protect their own best interests on large investments.

I might add that a good rep is at his best in this type of negotiation. He knows his product—and frequently knows the customer's operation—well enough to suggest an added advantage to your offer that will cost you little but increase the customer's satisfaction greatly. In one case our principal had the special expertise of a piece of equipment that could punch a hole in a forging. While eliminating a drilling operation by the customer, the action cost the company only slightly more to include in its processing. With this cost added to the price, the customer's overall cost was still less. We received the order because of our knowledge of our principal's capabilities and practical costing methods.

The rep must do his part by checking reaction to your pricing policies and providing intelligent feedback. Only through his efforts can you analyze your pricing structure as it relates to your competitors. Without knowing how high or low you are compared with other bidders, you may lose business through not making an adjustment in your manufacturing costs. On the other hand, you may gain business with pricing that is below the level needed to retain your share of the orders at a reasonable profit.

Make a Top-Quality Product

Purchasing agents will overlook a great many minor annoyances if a vendor supplies them consistently with a high-quality product. Receiving a shipment of badly needed goods and discovering they don't meet specifications drives most purchasing people to distraction and damages the credibility of your rep.

This disappointment in your performance is not limited to purchasing people. A poor-quality shipment in times of emergency creates turmoil throughout the entire customer organization. From the man on the line who may lose income because he has no work to do when production slows down, to the plant manager who faces cost increases because overhead continues despite the reduced production—everyone is affected. Needless to say, walking into a firm after this has occurred and facing all those hostile faces is an unpleasant experience for a rep. Although he has absolutely no control over the quality of a part, he's held responsible for the defect and his other lines suffer as a result.

In one case, word about a defective shipment from one of my companies had spread so far and wide throughout the territory that when I walked into the customer's office to face the music, several sales people in the reception room winked at me empathetically and one competitor could hardly keep from breaking into a broad grin. The customer's treatment of me that day was courteous but stern, and to its credit the firm has never personally held that expensive faux pas against my agency; we've been called in on other business there. Even the offending firm was given a second chance, but when the same defect occurred on a subsequent shipment, our business for that principal ended with that customer.

It doesn't take a rep long to gauge the quality of your company's performance, and it's likely that he'll check this factor out as thoroughly as he possibly can before he signs a contract with you. But this is not an easy task, particularly if you have little or no business in his area. He'll try to determine whether you have reps of his acquaintance in other territories, and contact them for references about your overall performance. I've made many such phone calls myself and found them most helpful—and usually most encouraging. It seems that companies long familiar with the rep game have profited from their early mistakes; most of the references I've received are favorable.

Good quality has effects beyond the immediate order; it both builds and fortifies the customer's belief that the supplier can be depended on to furnish an acceptable product year in and year out. Once such a reputation is established, it's hard for a competitor to lure the business away, even with a lower price.

A good part of my new business comes from buyers whose patience has been exhausted by a current supplier's repeated failures to meet their quality standards. Although as resistant to change as most humans are—and buyers are human, regardless of what some disillusioned salesmen may think—eventually they'll give up on a supplier who causes them constant irritation with inferior goods. Fortunately, by maintaining regular contact with such a customer on behalf of one or more of my principals, I've been able to detect this dissatisfaction and replace the offending supplier with a principal of mine that makes a competitive product.

A direct man, limited to selling your product only, will not have this day-to-day contact with a firm that's buying another's product. If he stops in at just the right time he may be able to take advantage of the customer's dissatisfaction with a competitor, but that will be a rare case of lucky timing. The rep, however, sensing a growing disenchantment with a competitor's quality performance, can subtly inform the buyer of the success he's had with your product at another local firm, even to the point of suggesting that the buyer here call the buyer there, thus cashing in on this chance opportunity to introduce your product.

If you're fortunate enough to secure an initial order, it should be red-tagged from the day it's received until the goods are delivered to the new customer. Murphy's law—which loosely declares that if something can possibly go wrong it will—is never more devastating than in the processing of the first order from a new customer, just when the rep wants so badly to prove that all the good things he's been telling the buyer about your firm are true. That's why you should make a special effort to check and recheck the quality of your product on that first order. If necessary, hand-walk it through the final processing to make sure it's right. Then, if the product is small enough, send a sample to your rep so he can personally give the purchasing people a firsthand look at the quality they can expect from you.

The first thing a buyer does when you show him your sample is get on the phone and ask engineering or quality-control people to come in and take a look at your version of a part that has been giving them trouble in the past. They'll examine the item very carefully, and if it's good your rep will be the hero of the day. If it's not, you can imagine your customer's chagrin as he anticipates a continuation of his sorry experiences. Make it right, but don't dandy it up to exceed your regular quality standards. The deception will be noticed when production parts are received, and the resulting anger and frustration will reflect poorly on your company's credibility.

The above procedure worked well for me recently with a customer who had been having quality problems with a casting supplier for years and was thinking of making a change. While I was visiting the purchasing agent one day on another matter, he mentioned that the company had lost over $100,000 of business as a result of poor quality and late deliveries on the part of its present supplier. I again reminded him of my principal, Oren Northcutt, who I was confident could solve his problem.

The purchasing agent reluctantly agreed to try five parts that made up an assembly for a switch on a valve, and in a few weeks I walked into his office with five samples. He grabbed the five parts and literally leaped from his chair and beckoned me to follow. We went straight to the manufacturing manager's office where a small crowd of technical experts quickly gathered. They minutely examined the parts with their micrometers, and smiles gradually appeared all around as they realized a major problem had been solved—the parts were perfect. No longer would they lose business from their customers because of poor quality.

Since that time we've shipped thousands of quality parts to this company and we expect a continuing business of approximately $70,000 a year. Oren circumvented Murphy's law by personally guiding these parts through his operation the first time around, thus assuring a satisfied customer from day one. Our customer is currently designing several more parts that we'll undoubtedly also make for him.

Oren's happy, I'm happy, and the customer's happy, all because a quality product is being made and all of us are profiting.

Attention to quality seems to be synonymous with the entrepreneurial instinct. Small companies that have grown into large ones are often headed by owners who were dissatisfied with the slipshod manufacturing practices and loose quality-control standards of the companies they worked for. They saw that the marketplace badly needed the same product in an improved version made with close attention to quality, and struck out on their own to take advantage of the ineffectual efforts of the current suppliers.

In the early years of operating a small firm founded on this premise, it's simple for the dedicated owner to insist on quality, because he can personally oversee the production and inspection operations. But when the company succeeds and grows larger—precisely because of this personal attention—a turning point is reached at which the owner must begin to delegate some of his responsibilities, including his day-to-day involvement in the production and quality-control processes that made his company successful. If at this juncture care isn't taken in selecting managers to head up these critical departments, all that he's strived for is in jeopardy.

Reps watch cautiously, and sometimes fearfully, as the nice small company they started doing business with begins to grow. Too often their fears prove to be well founded, as company after company fails to handle growth satisfactorily. Predictably, the first thing to fall off is quality. In the effort to pour more goods out the door, costs rise and previously rigid quality controls are loosened or ignored. Once proud of their product, company owners either are unable to select efficient managers or become enmeshed in pursuit of the dollar to the detriment of their own best interests. As quality goes downhill and the rejection rate mounts, the rep's enthusiasm wanes. He finds it unappetizing and unprofitable to devote his energies to selling a "clunker." So he turns to the firms that have maintained competitive quality standards and starts to neglect his wayward principal.

Another point at which many firms fail to make top-notch products is during a time of heightened demand. Because they must have the materials on hand to keep their production lines going, many purchasing and inspection people accept substandard quality just to get the items in their plant. Good companies won't accept goods that will make their own product structurally weak or dangerous, but they'll overlook the brightness of the finish of a part, the slight off-color appearance of a plastic component, or some other less-than-perfect condition. The supplier's shoddiness becomes the norm for future production—until the day when demand has lessened and a whole shipment of goods is rejected because of the same blemish that was accepted a few months earlier.

Fortunately, most companies have been through this cycle and are well aware of the pitfalls inherent in high-demand situations. They carefully avoid slipping into the habit of sacrificing in-plant control functions in favor of quick current dollars. Current dollars are important, but continuing dollars are the lifeblood of any company that intends to stay in business. Reps like to represent companies that show this determination, since their future is tied to their principals' future.

Provide Excellent Service

Quality of service has many subtle effects on your company's ability to hold a customer. One of the most important services is prompt delivery. If all companies lived up to their shipping promises, there'd be absolutely no need for expediters. This breed was developed during World War II when delivery of goods was vital to the war effort, but to this day companies haven't been able to eliminate the position.

Often your inability to ship on time is caused by your supplier's failure to ship to you on time. Other problems that make it impossible for you to meet your commitments are power failures and strikes. To help your rep in instances where you know you'll fail to meet your delivery promise, it's good practice to alert the rep and, of course, the customer. If sent sufficiently in advance, your warning will allow the customer to attempt adjusting his schedules to compensate for the late arrival of your product, as well as allow the rep to maintain his goodwill with the customer.

No notification is bad business. Over coffee the other morning, a rep in a neighboring office recalled his previous day's visit to a good customer. The buyer was angry. "After my fourth wire follow-up to your company," he said, "I still haven't received a firm promise on shipment of an order placed 16 months ago. I probably won't cut them off altogether in the future, but I placed an order yesterday with your competitor who's been trying to get my business for years."

This is discouraging news for a salesman, but particularly discouraging for a rep. A direct man can say, "Well, I'm sorry we're not delivering to this customer on time, but it's little or no money out of my pocket; I'll still get paid on Friday." The rep, on the other hand, not only has put up front money to solicit the customer's business, but will now experience a drop in his income because the customer has scaled down his purchases from the rep's principal.

Only a foolish rep will continue to vigorously pursue business for a principal who performs in this manner, particularly if it happens several times over. In this case the rep said, "To hell with them; they've lost business all over the territory because they can't even come close to their promises." This company stands to lose not only customers in the rep's territory but an excellent rep as well.

The future of the company's business here and perhaps elsewhere depends on its analysis of the reasons for the rep's disenchantment and eventual departure. It's possible that the sales manager neglected to make a prerecruitment analysis when he expanded his rep force. Perhaps the production department couldn't cope with the increased demand generated by their reps, or poor financial planning resulted in a cutoff of supplies by exasperated creditors. Perhaps the company should temporarily revert to a regional marketing plan and try to keep reps happy with prompt deliveries in their territories. In the meantime, the firm has financially penalized those reps who took seriously the promises of prompt deliveries to their customers.

Excellent service also means prompt responses to customers' questions, regardless of their importance or lack of it in your view. What matters is that they may be very important to your customer. Return mail replies will subconsciously make him aware that you're sensitive to his needs. Even the old trick of scribbling a reply on his original letter and sending him a photocopy will not offend—and will prevent piling up new loads of correspondence on your secretary's desk. Some companies even rubber-stamp a statement informing the customer that this method of replying is being used in the interest of a quick response.

Unanswered telephone calls irritate a buyer or a rep the most because this is almost a personal affront. A man who has taken the time and expense to place a call to your firm expects a return call promptly. A rule in our agency states that if we promise to call a customer back the following morning, we call him the following morning even if our principal hasn't yet been able to supply us with an answer. This policy assures our customers of our interest in their problems. I've made many a call along a noisy highway for just this purpose. A phone call from a customer means that his need is too urgent to communicate in a letter. If you treat it accordingly, he'll appreciate your prompt attention to his request.

A word about answering your rep's calls. His message, too, is important or he wouldn't be phoning. Promptness is doubly vital here because the rep's selling hours are limited and his stay in the office is short. The longer he waits for your response, the less time he can spend out in the field selling for you.

Our principals appear to have this well in hand. We receive speedy replies to our phone requests, and conclude from this experience that their customers are treated in the same fashion. (We've had no complaints to the contrary.) For routine calls to reps, most sales managers realize that Monday mornings and Friday afternoons produce the best results. Usually in their office preparing for the week's business or back from the field at these times, reps welcome any news about the business or answers to their letter or phone requests. The chance to keep in personal touch is important, including a word or two of encouragement now and then. Our egos don't need wholesale reinforcement, but an occasional massage does wonders.

Despite your best efforts, things do go wrong with your telephone communications. The cause frequently resides at the switchboard. A good example, not alarming but costly, was a long-distance call I placed to discuss some blueprint details with one of our sales managers. His line was busy, so, knowing it would take some time to find a copy of the print, I asked his receptionist to have him call me back after he had located the document. I gave her the print identification number and awaited his call.

He called back in five minutes, but when I asked him about a certain dimension on the print, he replied, "What print?" He promptly requested his engineering department to give him the drawing and expected to receive it in a minute or two. We killed time chatting; he called again for the print; and it finally arrived about ten minutes after he first requested it. His receptionist's diffident attitude to my request had meant that an ordinary $2.00 phone call probably cost more like $10.00.

While in this instance all it cost was money, an inefficient, rude, or unresponsive switchboard girl can lose you a customer. An efficient, intelligent, and courteous girl, on the other hand, can create oceans of goodwill. The whole personality of a company is reflected in the way the phone is answered and in the promptness and effectiveness of the effort expended to reach the person being called. I don't want to turn this into an essay on telephone manners; good information on this subject is free from the telephone companies. But I can't emphasize enough how critical good phone manners are to a favorable impression of your company.

A company that prides itself on good, attentive service toward all its customers, big or small, presents them with a unified picture of professional efficiency. Intercompany squabbles—accepted as inevitable—are kept within the confines of the company. Certain talented personnel who may be ineffective in interpersonal relations will be kept out of contact with the customer as much as possible. Here the rep can also be of assistance by sharing the knowledge he's gained of the capabilities of your people.

I often tell my customers the name of the person they should call if they need help or information from one of my principals. Knowing both parties, I can judiciously prevent problems from arising—and supplement my principal's efforts to keep relations smooth and feathers unruffled—by bringing together personalities that may be compatible with each other and keeping apart those that will definitely clash. For example, if a customer is really irate or disturbed, I may suggest a call to an executive who I normally would not bother with routine problems, but who I know will be able to handle the problem to the best possible advantage.

This is not an attempt to go over the head of the top manager's subordinates, but is rather a selective decision based on knowing the people involved and the further problems that could be generated by a call made through regular channels. This type of suggestion has always been made with considerable discretion, and the subordinates who may have been bypassed in a particular instance have always understood and accepted my reasoning.

Regardless of the magnitude of his contribution to your overall business, every customer should receive the impression that his orders are important to your company. By maintaining a consistent pricing policy, providing an excellent product, and getting it there on time, you're confirming the customer's feeling that you want his business and you're making his job easier. Just as essential is your prompt and courteous attention to his needs when a problem arises. Companies that treat their customers in so regal a manner will gladden the hearts of their reps as well—and a happy rep is an effective rep.

10

ADVERTISING, CUSTOMER RELATIONS, AND FIELD ASSISTANCE

The rep can't do it all

Asking a rep to do the entire job of selling your product in his area not only is unfair to him but will prove to be unproductive for you. Too many firms today are concentrating on good support programs to allow a nonparticipant any great success. With a little imagination, a little expense, and a lot of determination, you can develop a backup program that will effectively supplement your reps' work in the field.

The Importance of Advertising

In a survey made a few years ago by the trade association marketing staff of a major custom manufacturing industry, 49 percent of the respondents said their firm used advertising in the sale of their components. Unfortunately, that was as far as the survey went. No further information was requested about the type of advertising used by these companies.

From my experience with that industry, I'd guess that about 90 percent of the firms that advertised were using the Yellow Pages and/or the *Thomas Register,* a directory where products and manufacturers are listed alphabetically. Use of these media was no doubt defensive, since the first thing a salesman for either directory does in soliciting your business is to turn to the pages listing your industry and point out that most of your competitors have inserted some type of ad in that section. Usually these directories contain the most unimaginative ads to be found anywhere. Very few companies employ an advertising agency, and the choice of type, copy, and even illustrations is often left to the salesman's judgment.

In my experience as a rep I've found that only a small minority of firms have discovered the value of advertising. Most executives are results-oriented; they have to be, to insure a profitable operation of their company or department. If $100 is spent for a new calculator or $100,000 for a new machine tool, there must be evidence that the expenditure will ultimately return profits to the company. To these executives, advertising is an intangible. To spend $100 or $100,000 and see no measurable return is deeply disillusioning to them.

It's even more disillusioning to the entrepreneur who has had to jealously guard his available cash through the lean and difficult years of his modest enterprise. Every dollar was critical, and he undoubtedly made many mistakes in spending his money before coming out of the woods into solvency. He arrived at his current successful status through a lot of hard work and dedication that seldom included any popular form of advertising. Having established himself in the industry, he may have dipped into the till for a few hundred dollars and tried a modest advertising venture. Predictably, his expectations were much more grandiose than his results, and when little or no response was forthcoming he gave up in disgust. Or he simply may not believe in advertising, saying that the only way to be successful is through day-to-day contact with customers and prospective customers—and he's correct, to a degree.

No matter how clever it is, an advertising message can't be substituted for the personal contact needed to sell most products. Exceptions exist, such as mail-order programs and sophisticated telephone campaigns, but these are adaptable only to isolated products and will fail in general use.

The problem is that company managements frequently misunderstand the real purpose of advertising. They expect it to sell goods. Advertising seldom sells goods. Advertising is a supportive selling service; budgeting for this expenditure should be considered in the same light as a salesman's expenses. Without a car, a place to sleep and eat while on the road, and an entertainment allowance, a salesman would be working under an impossible handicap and couldn't do his job. Managements know this, so they provide their salesmen with these essentials.

All reps also need these supporting services and provide them for themselves, but I've noted that regardless of the size of the car or the entertainment budget, the more successful reps are working for companies whose names are familiar. This familiarity is a direct result of the effectiveness of their advertising. I'm an avid reader of almost any piece of literature I see in a customer's reception room. The collection usually consists of trade journals read by influential executives in the plant before being placed in the reception room.

Companies that advertise in these journals don't expect their readers to pick up the phone and place an order immediately after reading the advertisements. But they do expect—or at least hope—that when their sales people first call on a prospect, the spark of recognition generated by consistent advertising will make the purchasing agent listen a little more closely or even ask about some detail of the company's product that the ads have made him curious about.

Over the years the biggest plus I've received from some of our principals' advertising has been the buyer's acknowledgment that he's heard of my company. This recognition always gives me an initial advantage over a competitor whose company is not familiar to the buyer. I remember one occasion where I had finally convinced a purchasing agent that he should try my company's product. He agreed, but sighed, "It'll never get through engineering; they take forever to approve a new vendor." Two days later he phoned to tell me an order was on the way, adding in an astonished voice, "The chief engineer approved your company the minute I requested his O.K." In this case my principal has carried on a regular advertising campaign for years and years.

When I told him this happy story, the sales manager speculated that, through their constant exposure to his firm's advertising, industrial readers gradually have come to relate the company's name with quality. They actually believe they're familiar with the company's high standards, although they've had no previous personal contact with the company. Of course this strategy works only once—quality must be maintained if advertising is to continue to have this positive effect.

A Variety of Advertising Techniques

Many advertising and promotional techniques are available to help your rep in the field.

Brochures and technical literature. A brochure with your name on it is a must. Comprehensive files, by product classification, are kept by most good buying and engineering people. Larger companies actually employ a librarian to maintain up-to-date information on thousands of companies and their products.

A rep wastes his time if he must make a cold selling call with nothing to leave but his business card. A brochure can keep your company's name in the buyer's mind. It must be informative about your company's capabilities and should include technical information—we always leave two copies, asking the buyer to forward one to his technical personnel. Reps always carry a good supply of each of their principals' brochures on every call because they never know when a visit on behalf of one principal will lead to an inquiry about another; it happens over and over again.

In the case of catalogs illustrating standard products that you manufacture, it's necessary to show a little more discretion because of the increasing cost of producing these publications. One of our sales managers points out, however, that it costs more for the catalogs to sit on his shelf than on a customer's, so we spread them around.

When making a cold call we attempt to interest the buyer in the product we think he'll be most likely to purchase, but we also prepare a folder of secondary products that we believe might spark his appetite. If our initial probe draws little reaction, we may pull out this other folder and selectively go over the alternative items. But we're always careful not to flood him with material and thereby dilute his concentration on any one of our products. If he's interested in our initial presentation, we may not bring out any further brochures on this first visit, on the assumption that we may be able to offer our other products more intelligently and effectively as we come to know him and his company better.

This illustration makes clear that if one of our principals doesn't provide us with a brochure, it will lose out to principals that do supply literature—not because we don't want to sell their goods, but because they haven't given us enough supporting material to work with.

Technical bulletins. An article written by your personnel about some technical breakthrough by your company or in your industry can be very helpful to a rep. A buyer may be pleased to see us, but his time is valuable and purely social calls are becoming less welcome as pressures mount in these days of intense competition. Your reps will be delighted if you issue periodic technical literature that can give them a legitimate reason for a visit to a customer and perhaps a shot at an order.

Some products don't lend themselves to technical breakthroughs. If yours doesn't, consider an occasional case history of how a customer saved money by using your product in a unique fashion. Case histories are effective for two other reasons. (1) Often the customer whose story you're featuring will be very cooperative, and in working up a case study with his help you can discover other areas worthy of value analysis—utilizing your products, of course. (2) Your customer will be pleased by the publicity his product receives through your publication of his case study. It could mean increased sales for his company.

Direct mail. One of our more progressive principals sends out a monthly stock list of supplies on hand and supplementary mailings informing customers of technical and marketing news of interest both to them and to potential customers. Their secret—aside from the well-written and pertinent copy—is their mailing list. It's religiously kept current through a variety of techniques—for example, by prodding and encouraging reps to make corrections in personnel, titles, or addresses whenever and wherever they occur.

This is no mean feat, and it's a tribute to the company's executive management that it realizes the importance of an up-to-date mailing list. And why do we work so hard to help the company keep its list current? Because every so often a new order comes across our desk from a company we missed in our travels. We receive a commission regardless, so it's only fair (and good sense) that we contribute our time to assist the company in its continuing effort to conduct a good direct-mail campaign.

Direct mail is one of the most expensive methods of advertising and must be consistent to be successful. If you decide to try it, keep these two points in mind. (1) Before you begin, determine to budget sufficient funds for at least a one- to two-year trial period. (2) Budget your time to guarantee that your mailings go out regularly.

Some companies that effectively use direct mail forget to place their reps on the mailing list. This is an easy oversight, but it deprives your reps of an opportunity to discuss salient features of a mailing with a customer.

Trade journals. Many of the criteria employed in selecting a trade journal in which to advertise for reps can be used to determine the industry journals best suited to carry ads directed to your customers. The exception, of course, would be our original recommendation of a journal with a high readership among sales people. It stands to reason that you're now interested in reaching mostly purchasing and technical personnel; and, for example, if your product is capital equipment, you'll want to reach top management executives.

If your product serves several industries, however, you have a complicated task ahead, trying to allocate an equitable budget to the journals of each industry you serve. This selection can be made easier if you review your customer list and categorize each customer by SIC number. The SICs can be broken down into percentages of product sold to each SIC category, which will give you an indication of the different industries you serve and in what proportion.

Other factors, such as new products and new markets, will also govern your decision, and a good advertising agency can be a big help in your choice. Do remember, however, that with few exceptions you're more experienced in ascertaining potential customer demand than your agency. You should retain a large say in how your advertising dollar is allocated.

Following Up the Sales Lead

Aside from making the marketplace aware of your product, your trade journal advertising will please reps because many sales leads flow from ads that offer additional help to the reader through reader service cards. The reader can get more information by merely circling a number on the postage-free card inserted in the magazine and sending the card to the publisher, who forwards the inquirer's name to the advertiser. Success in following up these leads rests in your hands. If your rep doesn't receive the lead promptly, the customer may have forgotten why he asked for the information in the first place and a visit may be wasted. The rep should do his part also. To help us recognize the urgency of prompt follow-up, our agency date-stamps all leads received.

Paradoxically, you'll be doing your reps a favor if you avoid some journals known as "high inquiry producers." These are usually read by technical people who have a penchant for collecting everything and anything remotely connected with their company's product. Remember, it's the quality of sales leads that counts, not the quantity. Sometimes these journals can be pointed out to you by your advertising agency, or even by your reps after their many fruitless follow-ups.

As stated, we classify our sales leads when they're received. For example, we sell to a large manufacturer in Dallas that employs an inordinate number of design engineers because of its great variety of products. We get more leads from this firm than from the entire oil-tool industry, but sell only a small amount of goods to it. Making matters even more difficult, these engineers often ask that material be sent to a home address, possibly a company policy to discourage salesmen from disturbing personnel at the plants. We know one thing about the people, however—they do read a lot of magazines.

Our personal philosophy is that one good sales lead is worth five cold calls. A man who'll take the time to fill out and mail a request for literature will usually have some interest in the product he's seen described in the ad. Contrast this with the total shot in the dark when we cold call on a buyer or engineer who we think and hope will have some interest but who hasn't requested any information and may not even have heard of our principal.

The crossbreeding effect. A sales lead from one principal can turn into an inquiry about a product of one of our other principals. This happens so often that it's almost spooky, but it usually evens itself out among our companies, and each benefits from the other's sales leads. If owners and sales managers of firms employing direct men could spend a week or two with a rep, they'd see this crossbreeding effect in action and be astonished at how many opportunities are missed by a direct man.

We're constantly running across companies that are potential users of our principals' products where no evidence of their need is apparent. A recent example of this crossbreeding occurred when I followed up a request by a chief engineer for information on powdered-metal parts. He had been machining a part out of solid steel at great expense, thereby increasing the cost of the finished unit to the point where its price put it at a competitive disadvantage.

One look at the part told me it was unsuitable for the powdered-metal process, but was an ideal candidate for an investment casting of the type made by Oren Northcutt. After ironing out a few technical difficulties with its chief engineer, we received an order from this firm for a trial lot. The company currently purchases about $5,000 worth of this part every year. Its purchases of other similar parts may increase total business from this company by $10,000 to $15,000.

A direct man for a powdered-metal company would have walked away empty-handed. A direct man for a casting firm would never have been shown the part in the first place, since the chief engineer hadn't considered the part a potential casting. But as a rep with several options to offer, I was able to secure a new customer for Oren.

"Yes," you may say, "but what did the sales lead do for the powdered-metal company whose promotional efforts generated the original inquiry?" One call as a follow-up to this sales lead "normally" won't benefit this company, but a new relationship was created between the customer and myself as a result of my being able to reduce his costs through another principal, and he's likely to call on me first if he comes up with another part that looks as if it should be made as a powdered-metal component.

I said that's what "normally" would have occurred: no present order but a possibility later on. But in this case we discussed his unit further and he complained about another part that was giving him cost fits. When I saw it I knew it had definite possibilities as a powdered-metal part, and after a few modifications in dimensions are made we expect an order for this part also.

Such a success would have been very difficult without a sales lead. Although eventually I may have made a routine call at this company, I'd have probably received only casual attention from the purchasing agent, who might not even have been aware of the chief engineer's problems.

Sales leads need reviewing and culling, but one good order can make it all worthwhile. Leads and reps go well together.

The Importance of Customer Relations

Business relationships are hard to build up and all too easy to tear down. The typical ending of a relationship with a customer is gradual and stems more from neglect than from one particularly damaging action. Customers are a bit like friends. They like to know you care but don't want to be smothered with attention.

It's the rep's job to provide the right amount of concern and attentiveness, but a reasonable amount of looking after has to come from the principal. If your customer senses that only the rep pays attention to him and he and the rep have to form an alliance to demand good service from you, you'll eventually lose him, and possibly your rep. The alliance should be the other way around. The customer must be convinced that you and the rep are working together to keep him satisfied.

A number of things can be done to establish this rapport, but consistency is again a vital ingredient. A monthly or quarterly newsletter of some type can be sent to your regular customers. A different customer can be featured in each issue. A story on that company's products, on how successful the company has been, and on how your firm and your rep have played an important role in keeping it competitive and enabling it to deliver its goods on time—this kind of attention will provide you and your customer with a sense of partnership.

Including a few features about your company and its people will also make the customer feel closer to your organization. Incorporating provisions for routing on the first page will allow the purchasing agent to forward the newsletter to other personnel when he's finished reading it. Your agency or a particularly qualified printer can help you with a timely publication. You should enlist the help of your reps in ferreting out stories that will interest customers in his area and that give him an occasional printed pat on the back—they do wonders for his morale.

Several other techniques can be used to show your interest. (1) A follow-up call or card after a particularly critical delivery requirement is met will determine whether or not the product arrived in good shape. (2) An occasional mailing with several questions on a self-addressed return card can determine if service has been satisfactory and if there are any complaints not previously voiced. (3) A thank-you card can be mailed every so often. I get one of these included in my bill from my insurance agent. This happens about twice a year and I remember it. (4) A small, useful gift to personnel at your customers' plants will be appreciated—and if you want to make a special impact, send it at some time other than the Christmas season. (5) If you spot a news item that would be of special interest to one of your customers or someone in his plant, clip it and send it along with a short note. One of my sales managers sent a customer a copy of a newspaper article about the stellar performance of the customer's product in a Philadelphia suburb. The customer would never have seen this article and was highly flattered to think that the sales manager would be that thoughtful.

I could go on with innumerable examples, but these few should inspire you with a number of ideas that may be particularly apt for your own company or industry.

Consistent careful attention to your customers' needs will complement your reps' efforts, and you'll be on the road to long, continuing excellent business relationships unless you make the one fatal mistake that can undo everything you've done. That mistake involves the handling of phone and mail contacts with your customers. The wrong personnel in a position of personal contact can so irritate the customer that all the good relations you've painstakingly established with him can be completely erased.

Our more successful principals have carefully selected the inside people who deal with their customers. These skilled diplomats work constantly at the delicate chore of saying the right things to all customers, even when refusing a request. They attempt to reply promptly either by phone or by mail, to have as much information as possible at their fingertips, and to keep harmony within the ranks at their own company. This is a herculean task, and managements that have the foresight to hire these specialists and pay them well are aware of the importance of the sales correspondent's function.

This attitude must of course extend to other departments. A production control man who once worked for me had been badgered by an unreasonable expediter until he could stand it no longer. He sent a fiery letter to the expediter outlining all the impossible demands and changes that had been requested, and stopped just short of telling him what to do with his business. When our rep got his copy of this rude letter he was immediately on the phone to me, rightly complaining. It took all the collective efforts we could muster to hold on to that customer.

When confronted with the effects of his temper tantrum, the production control manager saw immediately that his impulsive action had almost cost us a good customer, regardless of the justness of his feelings. He had reached the position of production control manager through the many skills he had learned over the years; this experience in public relations was absorbed in the same fashion, with the result that his later letters became fine examples of courteous correspondence.

Clearly, the most important aspect of your customer relations will be the impression you make in your day-to-day communications with your customers. When your rep thinks you're handling these contacts satisfactorily, he'll confidently refer his customers to you for quick, efficient answers rather than route every query through his own office to reduce the danger of antagonizing a valuable customer. He can then concentrate his total efforts on selling, which is exactly why you hired him.

The Importance of Field Assistance

A periodic visit to the territory by the sales manager or some sales-oriented executive can be a real aid to the rep. You may have a buyer on the verge of purchasing from your principals but some inexplicable reservation is holding him back. In my opinion this compulsion to delay making decisions as long as possible—particularly decisions requiring change—is built into everyone's personality. The appearance on the scene of a company man with substantial authority, however, seems to ease a buyer's reluctance to act. He feels that if the company has enough interest in him to send its executives on regular visits, it's definitely interested in the area and will service it well.

I recently had a discussion with a talented sales manager whose boss may have been having some doubts about his sales representative force. "We get inquiries from the reps and a few orders," the boss had commented to him, "but when *you* visit the territories things really begin to happen." The boss was absolutely right in this particular case. His product is custom-made and relatively sophisticated. The reps have been successful in generating a lot of interest and a considerable amount of business, but when the sales manager is in the territory they arrange for visits to firms whose buyer they've brought as far as he'll go without some further evidence of company interest.

In addition, this sales manager has on-the-spot authority to say yes or no on an engineering point and can often swing the firm to his side by a good technical dissertation on a vexing problem. Consequently, the chips fall into place as the visiting executive makes call after call.

Having been through the ordeal of cold calling day after day with maybe one out of 20 visits showing some promise, a perceptive sales manager recognizes the rep's contribution to the good results of these team calls. The rep has done a lot of spadework and homework, and this teaming up of sales manager and rep can accomplish quite a bit in a short visit.

Of course the perceptive rep also realizes the value of these field trips. He knows that without the sales manager's regular visits there'd be some accounts he'd never crack, so he appreciates and encourages scheduled trips to his territory by company executives.

Sales managers get the best results out of their trips to the field through intelligent scheduling. By planning three to four weeks in advance whenever possible, they give their reps an opportunity to bring the important accounts to a point where as many of the sales manager's calls as possible will be timed to coincide with a buying or engineering decision. Naturally, this isn't always possible, but a field trip planned well in advance will surely bring more rewarding visits than one planned on Friday for the following week.

Of course an emergency trip is occasionally necessary because of a customer's problem or request for assistance. When this happens, full advantage should be taken of the company man's presence in the area. Visits to other customers in the area are always worthwhile, even when made on such short notice.

Don't make a field trip, then go home with all kinds of inquiries and requests from customers and potential customers, and finally neglect them in favor of more pressing duties at the office. At this point you have a golden opportunity to develop business in the rep's area and keep his morale high. Nothing is more shattering to a rep than to leave a company man at the airport—arms loaded with prints, inquiries overflowing from his briefcase, and enthusiastic promises of prompt action on his lips—and then watch the mails for weeks without seeing any response. Giving immediate priority to anything that has come up during your visit will keep your rep out searching for new accounts in anticipation of your next visit.

This is not to suggest that reps are incapable of bringing in most of the business on their own; if so, there wouldn't be much need for them. But combining talents in this way at the right time triggers a team spirit that brings in business the rep may not be able to obtain alone. His customers are usually a long way from your plant, and your regular appearances signify serious interest in their welfare. Our principals who don't travel the area with us seem to do the least business—I think that result speaks for itself.

One final note on field trips. If your product requires engineering expertise—rather than being a standard or stock item—it's essential that technical personnel be permitted and encouraged to visit the customer whenever such a request is made, by either the customer or the rep. Some small but nagging problem can be blown all out of proportion by a company's refusal to hastily dispatch an engineer or quality-control expert to placate and service an unhappy customer. And while he's in the territory, spending an extra day or two accompanying the rep in his visits to technical personnel at the plants of other customers is always an effective use of time.

A rep's ability to produce is limited to an extent by the performance of your backup support. You can considerably increase your power to motivate him by following the basics outlined in this chapter. Consistent support is necessary for a good all-round customer assault. The rep can dig out prospects, tell them about you, try to sell them your product, and succeed in many cases. But his success can be dramatically increased by an enterprising program of advertising, customer relations, and well-planned field trips.

11

CALL REPORTS, FORECASTS, AND QUOTAS

Surviving the paper blizzard

The paperwork mania that pervades modern-day business has worked mightily against the salesman. Companies use sophisticated psychological testing techniques to find sales people who are gregarious, love activity, and abhor detail, then turn around and demand voluminous reports on all aspects of their activities. Frequently it's expected that this paperwork be prepared after the evening meal, adding two or three hours to the salesman's day.

One of our nation's largest firms has a local office in Dallas that provides absolutely no desk space for its sales people here. The salesman is expected to appear at the office only for a sales meeting or to pick up his messages, which the firm encourages him to do by phone. Yet the salesman has to submit a complete report on every sales lead or assignment, in writing.

Although I have no figures to back me up, I'd guess that a study would show a significant negative correlation between the amount of paperwork required and the volume of sales per salesman. Anticipating writing a report or other analysis on each call subconsciously acts as a deterrent to a salesman making calls. He knows that each appearance in a customer's office means another piece of paperwork.

This negative effect is particularly strong when a paperwork-oriented firm decides to begin marketing its products through reps. If its new reps are expected to submit regular call reports, provide detailed forecasts, and enthusiastically embrace a sales quota, the company might as well throw in the towel. These expectations must be compromised right from the beginning or the firm's rep program will be in disarray in short order. However, by careful planning and with some knowledge of the workings of a typical rep force, a sales manager can succeed in receiving helpful information from his reps.

Call Reports—Avoid Them

As a sales manager I never sought formal call reports from my reps, and as a rep I have never received a request for them from my sales managers. A close friend who owns a small manufacturing company recalls the early days of his rep recruitment program when he wrote a clause into his rep sales agreement stipulating that call reports be submitted on a regular basis. He couldn't understand the fuss kicked up by the reps about this minor (to him) requirement.

He reasoned that salesmen should detail their calls for several reasons: to make sure they're making their required calls, to learn as much as possible about how the company's product is accepted in the field, and to compile a written record for each customer. His error was in failing to realize that most salesmen look on these reports as control devices. He was striking at a raw nerve when, by inserting this call report clause, he intimated that he sought regular control over his reps. The rep is a rep because he treasures his independence; he rebels against any formal attempt at control.

If you can get away from the formal nature of many requests for information, you'll doubtless receive cooperation from most professional reps. They realize that feedback from the field is necessary and are aware that without this feedback they can hardly expect you to take corrective action on procedures that are causing you to lose business.

You *will* run into resistance, however, if you request regular reports of any kind. Here they sense that their correspondence will be treated routinely, perhaps reviewed superficially and then placed in a file somewhere. Whether this is true or not in your particular case, you can gather much more pertinent data by making requests only when there appears to be an honest need to know some particular details about a customer or a competitor. In this case the benefit that such information will bring to the company is evident.

On many occasions I've been asked for information on certain firms in our territory and gladly spent as much time as necessary digging up the details requested. These requests can range from the names of executives to be included in a direct-mail program to information outlining the extent of penetration of a competitor's product in the area.

My partner and I also write a number of unsolicited call reports every week. We try to keep our principals informed about their customers when we discover an item of information that we know will be of interest. We both carry portable tape recorders, and while we don't use them in a customer's office, we may record our thoughts before we leave the company's parking lot. This is easier and more efficient than attempting to jot down notes. If a few minutes later we think of something at first forgotten, we can record again at the next stoplight.

Although you can't expect to receive regular call reports, you should expect to receive letters and phone calls from your rep giving you current pertinent information about your customers. Reps who don't attempt to provide this type of communication are not doing the job and should be reminded of their obligation to keep you informed on any developments at a customer's plant. You'll receive prompt informational reports from the professional rep by reminding him that without intelligent feedback from the field you can't take corrective action.

Forecasts—Make Them Honest

No company can plan ahead without some estimate of its future volume of business. Capital expenditures must be made carefully lest they be undertaken without the influx of new orders needed to justify the risk of purchases. Progressive managements operate within budgets that are established at the beginning of the year through careful analysis of the projected amount of business for that year. To facilitate this planning, the sales department must be able to forecast sales accurately. This requires honest appraisals by everyone, from the people in the home office to the most far-flung rep. The key word is "honest," and getting such appraisals is more difficult than it seems at first it would be.

Once, when we had our franchised rug-cleaning business, we were alerted by the franchising company's executive in charge of sales development that he'd be in town soon and that he expected our sales and profit forecast for the coming year. We analyzed the economic conditions, the negligible and deteriorating promotional help from the franchising company, and our overall operations, and drew up a forecast that showed a reduction in sales volume and income for the next year.

Upon arrival, the executive took one look at our forecast and angrily declared it unacceptable. "How can anyone who expects to succeed in business prepare a forecast showing a reduced volume for the year ahead?" he asked. Part of our strategy in making such a forecast had been to point out the deficiencies in the franchising company's advertising and promotional support of our efforts. But while he may have secretly agreed with our forecast, the executive could not return to his home base with such a forecast for presentation to the president of his firm. So, our point made, we changed our forecast to a glowing appraisal of the year ahead and left the executive at the airport in a much relieved condition. However, the year's results turned out almost exactly in line with our original forecast.

This is the problem with most forecasting. Unless a company's sales management is allowed to present its owners, board of directors, or stockholders with the "honest" outlook for the next year, the sales group will be obligated to come up with an increase in each year's forecast in spite of adverse selling conditions. It's always easy to project an increase in volume; no one argues with you, and if you should fall short a variety of reasons can be cited to explain the discrepancy; but this is obviously a short-sighted policy and can lead a naive or demanding management to grievous errors in planning and expenditures.

Such a disastrous possibility can be avoided, in my view, if, prior to asking for a forecast, managements would provide sales departments with a reasonable forecast of the economic climate and other factors that could influence the year ahead. The proposed introduction of a new product or the obsoleting of another could be factors that would influence a forecast. Armed with this knowledge—which should of course be passed on to the reps—everyone is in a better position to look ahead and develop an honest prediction of what will happen in the course of the year ahead.

We reps are not economists, but through our close relationship with our customers we're often able to sense an upturn or downturn in their business, sometimes even before they're aware of it themselves. We visit different departments in our pursuit of sales, and can observe an engineering department becoming less active or a steady inventory buildup that's not being worked off as rapidly as it should. These observations can be meaningful to the perceptive rep, and his assistance should be enlisted in preparing your forecast. Be sure he understands that his contribution is only part of the whole. If he knows that he'll be allowed to be wrong, or that he can project a decrease in volume without being terminated, he'll do his best to cooperate in judging the future flow of business.

This past year we erred badly in forecasting for several of our principals. Knowing there was an energy crisis and that a fair portion of our business is from oil-tool firms, we looked forward to a good year. We had no way of anticipating that Congress would drastically alter the oil depletion allowance. Customers involved in selling to domestic drillers were temporarily forced to curtail their purchases, thus adversely affecting the predictions we had confidently made of continuing orders from these oil-tool firms.

Except for our concern over diminishing commissions, we were not unduly worried about the reactions of our principals to our erroneous forecasts. They had impressed us from the start with their ability to understand the hazards of crystal-ball gazing twelve months into the future. One of our rep acquaintances, however, represents a firm that publishes a monthly analysis of sales versus forecasts. This is sent out companywide in an ill-conceived attempt to spur the reps on to fulfill their forecasts. Since so many elements are involved in purchases by customers, it's almost impossible to predict month-to-month sales figures; consequently, the report serves more to embarrass reps than to stimulate them to greater action. This use of forecasting is damaging and works against the principal-rep relationship.

Depending on the number of customers you have in a rep's area and the amount of paperwork involved, forecast time is often an opportunity to find out a great deal about your customers' intentions for the coming year. If your rep is asked for his forecast well in advance, he can start compiling information as he makes his routine rounds. He can seek renewals of blanket orders—that is, orders for products for a given period in advance—and these will serve as a barometer of expected business volume. He can probe the optimism or pessimism of buyers and purchasing agents, and can investigate the possibilities of customers' design changes, often an indication of a tightening competitive situation.

You should encourage your reps to estimate the outlook of local business conditions. Often a specific area will have an economic climate that deviates from general economic trends. For instance, during much of the '74–'75 recession, Odessa, Texas, reported an unemployment rate of under 4 percent, a figure that would have been even lower if housing had been available for needed workers. Yet the country's rate went over 9 percent, and rates in some localities were as high as 20 percent. Information of this type, if available sufficiently in advance, can drastically affect your marketing strategy for a planned period and mean the difference between a profit and a loss year.

Forecasting is an important management tool. If its usefulness is made apparent to all who are asked to burn the midnight oil preparing as accurate a prediction as possible, you'll receive—and you should insist on receiving—a considerable amount of cooperation from all parties, including your reps.

However, if these contributors get the impression that the requested forecast is just so much additional paperwork that will be filed routinely along with other inconsequential data without having been carefully analyzed, then their replies will reflect this impression. They'll add 10 or 20 percent to last year's figures and let it go at that. If you can convince your personnel that the planning for next year's expenditures, hiring, expansion, and other actions affecting your ability to operate profitably depends on their accurate forecasts, you'll be able to accept the figures submitted as conscientious appraisals of future business.

Quotas—A Rep's Bugaboo

Dick Berry, a management specialist, listed 15 techniques used by companies to motivate their reps.* In his poll of reps, three of these motivators were tied for last place in effectiveness: fear, contests, and quotas. The motivating techniques at the top of the list were high commissions, product training, and the reputation of the principal, which included judgments on its product quality, backup, and support. In my own RepSurvey, only 23 percent of the respondents said they were

---

* "Motivating the Manufacturers' Agent," *Agency Sales*, February 1973, pp. 8–11.

required to meet quotas, and 80 percent of this group said that quotas didn't help them sell better.

Evidently, attempting to motivate reps by assigning quotas is like trying to swim upstream. By recalling the portrait of a sales rep sketched in Chapter 2, you'll quickly see why quotas are ineffective with this group. Independent, self-disciplined, ambitious, entrepreneurial men hardly need such a contrived goal to spur them to greater sales; it would in fact be more likely to dissuade them from making a really fine effort.

Aside from the psychological drawbacks to quota systems, every intelligent salesman knows that too many variables go into winning an order to make the technique feasible. Setting a dollar quota goal for reps is like setting quotas when planting a vegetable garden: you know most of the vegetables will come up, but exactly when and how many depends on conditions over which you have no control—wind, rain, sun, and temperature.

While I've been frankly critical of the quota system, I'm certainly in sympathy with the sales manager who's under pressure to continue the upward spiral of sales volume. The quota system, however, is an easy way to pass on the blame for failure in advance. A sales manager can take a sales rep's volume last year, tack on whatever percentage increase the company has set as its goal, and lean back to watch the action, secure in the knowledge that if results fall short he can fault the field sales force. A year or two of lagging sales will of course prompt management to take a closer look at the sales department's incentive methods; if the quota system has been heavily relied on for rep motivation, a new sales manager may soon appear on the scene.

Knowing the futility of assigning quotas to their reps, imaginative managers will work hard at other incentive programs. As Berry showed in the study mentioned earlier, however, this involves some factors that are beyond the sales manager's control: the reputation of his firm and its product quality. Here he has to convince his management that these factors will very definitely motivate reps; in fact, the whole organization has to appreciate the important role quality and reputation play in insuring a good order flow from the field.

There are other motivating techniques the sales manager can employ. He can see that information is disseminated regularly, and can insist that his department provide the rep force with good backup in matters of quotations and customer relations. When these basic techniques have succeeded, you can attempt additional incentive programs. I say attempt, because there are no sure things in rep incentive programs. What works for one company or one group of reps will not work for another; and even then, none of the programs I've participated in have met with more than mediocre success for our principals.

Contests pitting one rep against another are certain to cause problems and dissatisfaction in the ranks. A Midwest manufacturer using this device sends its entire rep group a monthly report ranking *all* reps' culminative sales performance for the year versus quota. Thus one agency heads the list, the others trail behind, and one firm inevitably has to be last. What makes the whole effort so transparent and so frustrating is that the older, more successful reps are assigned higher quotas each year and the newer reps much lower figures. Thus the new men appear near the top of the list each month and the proven producers bring up the rear.

By rigging the results to spur on and even shame veteran reps into a vigorous effort to "make quota," the firm is fooling only itself. The newer reps, naturally encouraged by their initial showing, soon become veterans and lose their enthusiasm because of the manner in which they were exploited earlier. This company also publishes a monthly report on the number of new accounts generated by each rep. At the last sales meeting a rep friend received the top award for obtaining 14 new customers in the previous year. Five months later he was replaced by a direct man.

Incentives for your reps cannot follow a "contest" philosophy. These men couldn't care less whether some other rep makes more sales. Their own success, reflected in the commissions they receive, matters most to them. A Cleveland company, however, uses a point system in a novel manner that does seem to work to a degree. They send their reps a merchandise catalog with the worth of each item shown as a point figure. On receipt of an inquiry from a firm not previously quoted, the rep is awarded 1,000 points. If the rep follows up the quotation within two weeks, he gets anothr 1,000 points. And if an order is received as a result, additional points are given, increasing with the dollar value of the order. The rep may then use these points to acquire a toaster, a watch, or whatever he wants, depending on the number of points he's accumulated.

This isn't a particularly new form of incentive, but it provides a little extra compensation without constantly ranking each rep in a contest. It also tends to reinforce one of Dick Berry's main motivating techniques: high commissions. While cash is the basic necessity, substitute forms of monetary reward may act more toward stimulating your reps than "psychological" substitute incentives that work with direct men—for example, personal recognition, contests, and quotas.

12

THE SALES MEETING

A boom or a bomb?

Approximately 50 percent of the companies employing reps conduct sales meetings. If your company is not among this group you may be shortchanging yourself. Planned and conducted with imagination, the sales meeting can prove to be one of the best motivational tools you have. A good sales meeting should improve and update the reps' product knowledge, provide a forum for good firsthand feedback from the field, acquaint your company's personnel with the reps who are working for them in the field, and keep the reps' enthusiasm high for your company and its products.

By not holding regular sales meetings you may be losing out to the reps' other principals who use this method to maintain the reps' concentration on their products. If a company doesn't conduct sales meetings or offer comparable field assistance, it deprives itself of the vital personal contact that is the very core of good rep relations and it almost certainly guarantees an unimpressive record of reps' sales.

It's surprising how many firms conduct business without this contact. In many instances the sales manager or owner may not even have met some of the company's reps. It's no wonder that firms with such an uninspired sales philosophy so often have a poor attitude toward reps, preferring to sell their products regionally because a half-hearted attempt at national selling through reps didn't bring the desired results.

The Wrong Way and the Right Way

One main deterrent to regular sales meetings is the expense involved, which can be considerable. This is another reason why you should proceed slowly with the recruitment of reps. A small company that hires 10 or 12 reps within a short period can't possibly afford the additional expense of an annual sales meeting for at least several years. It'll take that long for the reps to build the firm's business to the point where funds are available for such an expenditure. By beginning slowly with plant visits, field visits, and sales meetings, it's possible to give your new reps excellent assistance within a reasonable budget.

A poorly planned sales meeting is a complete waste of money. These meetings should not be a mere gathering of the flock for fun and games or for pep talks by the firm's president and executives. This not only is unrewarding to the reps but can dampen their enthusiasm for future meetings and reduce their interest in your firm's products and programs. However, a good, professionally run sales meeting enhances your image with the reps and sends them back to the field armed with new product knowledge and a feeling of confidence in your company's sales aims.

To be successful in planning for your rep sales meeting you'll have to assume a slightly different attitude than that needed in planning a similar meeting for direct men. Direct sales people are a captive audience and can be handled in a style of your choosing. I know many direct sales people who dread their weekly or monthly meetings, not necessarily because they begrudge the time, but because of the monotony of each meeting's subject matter and presentations. Too often a sales manager takes a pedestrian approach toward meetings with salesmen who must attend, must do as he instructs, must follow predetermined quota systems, and must conform to a host of other musts. The sales manager who can overcome this built-in trend toward inertia because his audience is captive deserves a hearty pat on the back.

An entirely different concept is necessary for a rep sales meeting. Your audience will consist of professional sales people who have attended many sales meetings over the years, some bad, some good, and some truly outstanding. Once again you're in a competitive situation. Your meeting will be compared favorably or unfavorably with others, and no sales manager wants to be remembered for putting on a meeting that didn't produce a feeling of enthusiasm among the attendants.

To insure success you'll need to start your plans well ahead of time and develop a program that will maintain high interest throughout the entire meeting. It can be done easily and effectively if you keep in mind that your reps are there to learn more about you, your company, your company's products, and how, through cooperative effort, more sales can be obtained in the coming year. A tour through a new plant or a relaxing day of golf or tennis is fine and gives a boost to the camaraderie that should be encouraged, but the main thrust must be aimed at imparting as much knowledge as possible within the few days you're all together.

When I was young I used to marvel at the way my father was able to speak extemporaneously. He'd get up in front of groups at school or at public affairs and speak freely and easily about whatever subject was under discussion. His delivery was smooth and effective. When I grew up and had to give my first business speech I assumed, from watching him, that a brief review of the subject matter would be sufficient preparation. I expected my words to flow with an inherited competency that would leave my audience amazed at my grasp of the subject and delighted with my ease and proficiency of presentation.

Well, I stumbled around, forgot most of what I was going to say, and put on a pretty miserable demonstration of what was supposed to be an informative address. It occurred to me on later reflection that my father had spent many an hour in his office in our home, no doubt extensively researching his subjects and preparing his presentations with the utmost care. His speeches were extemporaneous only in that he didn't use notes; he had firmly established in his mind exactly what he was going to say.

So it is with sales meetings. All the knowledge in the world will be of little avail if you haven't carefully planned your entire meeting and made it a smooth and informative day or two of concentrated learning experiences. Merely to gather a group of reps together and "kick things around" will be a disastrous waste of valuable time. Each leader and speaker must be aware of how important his contribution is to the whole and should be made to plan his part carefully.

So Do It the Right Way

Let's now briefly consider the essential elements of a successful rep sales meeting. By planning your meeting with full awareness of the importance of the elements discussed below, you can increase your odds of putting on a worthwhile and profitable presentation.

Frequency. Unless you're marketing regionally and your reps are fairly close to the home office, a yearly sales meeting will suffice. Though many firms seem content to schedule their meetings sporadically, you should try to be consistent. Random scheduling is usually a function of expense. Sales meetings are costly; therefore the tendency is to have these get-togethers in good years when volume and profits are up and to dispense with them during years of slower activity. This policy is somewhat irrational, since the basic goal of a meeting is to generate more sales. You should fight the paradox of conducting meetings when sales are up and eliminating them when the need is the greatest.

Ideally, a financial reserve should be set aside from good years to provide for meetings during poor years. Unfortunately, tax laws discourage this sort of financial planning. But sales meetings are too important to eliminate, so steps should be taken to hold them even in lean times. You can do this by planning a streamlined, cost-cutting meeting—cramming as much as possible into a short time by getting to the meat of the presentations and avoiding frills. Reps will understand an abbreviated session and will appreciate your attempt to keep them informed.

Another alternative is a small regional get-together led by one or two company people at a location where three or four reps can meet with a minimum of expense. You can compensate for these economy binges by having a bigger and wider-ranging gathering in better years.

Your meeting should be at a regular time each year with dates firmed up as far in advance as possible. A direct salesman can be summoned on short notice more easily than a rep who attends four or five meetings a year, travels his area for weeks with different sales managers and almost incidentally tries to sneak in a few weeks of vacation. That rep will need all the advance notice you can provide. One of our principals schedules a sales meeting every February and is always given top priority in our own scheduling because of its consideration in allowing us to make our travel plans well in advance.

Expenses. I've never attended a sales meeting held by one of our principals and been asked to pay any portion of my expenses. However, among the reps included in my RepSurvey, 60 percent of those who attended sales meetings paid their own travel costs. This discretionary policy depends on a number of considerations, the most important of which is the distance the reps have to travel.

Traditionally, the further away the territory is from the company, the less the company sells in that area. This means lower commissions for the rep who travels the greatest distance to and from home base. This may not make the trip worth his while, particularly if he's a capable rep and his lower sales are mainly due to higher freight costs or other disadvantages resulting from the greater distance of his operations from the company's production center.

Not only can reps closer to your plant sell your goods more competitively and thus in greater quantity with commensurate commissions, but they're asked to pay the least in travel expenses, which is not equitable. In addition, a travel allowance consisting of a portion of the expense is hard to administrate fairly and causes further hard feelings and confusion. I'm convinced that it's better to have meetings at less frequent intervals and pay all travel expenses than to have them more often and ask the reps to pay their own way.

Regardless of that arrangement, once the reps are at the meeting location all meal and lodging expenses should be assumed by the company. And by all means, give each rep his own room. Some of us snore, some keep irregular hours, others like to retire early, and still others need extensive use of the phone in off-hours to keep tabs on business at home. We'd rather have less pretentious accommodations but our own room than stay at a prestigious watering place and be asked to share a room with another rep.

Other expenses connected with the meetings—for example, green fees for a golf outing and diversions planned by the company—should be paid by the firm. Of course reps fully expect to cover expenses not connected with the meeting, such as a night on the town or rental of a car to visit a local friend or acquaintance.

Location. Convenience is obviously a major factor—and I'm speaking of convenience for the firm, not the rep. Most locations are within a few hours' flying distance of any part of the country, so it's not difficult for reps to travel to almost any spot you choose. However, if you've updated your production facilities or you're planning a tour of your plant for other reasons, then a location as close as possible to the production site is desirable.

I would recommend against holding meetings right at the company headquarters unless your plans require the reps' presence to observe some part of your operation. I've attended meetings at home offices and seen them constantly interrupted because company executives are available for emergency calls. The executive leaves the room in the middle of his presentation and 10 or 15 reps and assorted company people sit around with nothing to do until he returns. These interruptions are less numerous when the meeting is held at a motel or hotel located away from the office. A meeting leader can still be called to the phone, but a strong attempt should be made to discourage calls except during break times or the luncheon period.

Today's better hotels and motels are well equipped with meeting facilities, but make sure that you'll receive the manager's or program director's close cooperation during the course of your meeting. And carefully select the room you'll be using. A room I once rented for a late afternoon meeting was separated from an adjoining room by a sliding plastic partition; the meeting was progressing well when the sound of voices from the next room began intruding at a steadily increasing volume. The noise of the party that was taking place was distracting the attention of our audience almost completely just at the time the principal speaker was beginning his presentation.

A number of good sources of information on sales meetings are available to help you avoid making any such mistakes in choosing locations, and I can't emphasize enough how important thorough planning in this respect is to the ultimate success of your meeting.

If there's no particular reason for having your meeting near the company's headquarters, then a location more generally accessible to your reps can mean more convenience for all concerned and can save on travel expense, provided you don't have to bring along too many home-office people or ship in large products for demonstration. A good resort location is always popular and adds an informality that's conducive to a friendly and outgoing exchange of information between reps and company people.

When and how long? Unless he's a hopeless workaholic, no rep is fond of spending a weekend at a sales meeting. However, reps normally don't object to spending a Saturday or a Sunday attending a meeting; they just prefer not to give up both days.

For example, by planning a check-in on Sunday afternoon with an informal dinner meeting that evening, you allow the rep to leave home for the meeting site on Sunday morning. My experience has shown the Sunday evening starting time to work very well. Except for the perpetual playboys, your reps will be satisfied with an informal get-together Sunday evening and will be happy to retire at a reasonable hour, making them alert and receptive to your Monday morning kickoff. Ending a meeting on a Saturday somehow seems less effective, since everyone is anxious to leave and it's hard to maintain the weekday concentration into the weekend.

If at all possible, avoid scheduling your meetings for the middle of the week, since this cuts deeply into a rep's selling time. If he attends five meetings a year, that many weeks are eliminated from his selling schedule. A day or two at either end of the week still leaves him with two or three selling days in that week and allows him the continuity of contact he needs to stay on top of his business.

The time of year is also important. Because of vacations, summer is no time to attempt a meeting. Holiday seasons are equally bad, since reps and the personnel of his principals will have family or vacation plans. This leaves spring, fall, and part of winter. That's why I stress setting your meeting date as far in advance as possible: reps must work harder during the very periods that are best for sales meetings, and you must plan early to guarantee a well-attended meeting.

If you plan a two-day meeting, you're in accord with the preference of your peers. RepSurvey results showed 58 percent of the principals who hold sales meetings plan them for a full two days, 21 percent prefer one day only, 18 percent manage three days, and only 3 percent plod through four or more days.

A well-conducted two-day affair, tightly scheduled, is usually sufficient to allow a group of reps to absorb what you have to offer. Running over into the third day prompts participants to make more phone calls to their offices as messages pile up and customers await answers about quotes, shipments, and other day-to-day details. Concentration noticeably slackens, and you run the risk of losing the fine edge you carefully built up over the preceding two-day period.

Occasionally, if your meeting is held in conjunction with a trade show, your reps may wish to remain an extra day but will want to devote that time visiting the exhibits rather than spend it at a meeting. If your own firm is exhibiting, it sometimes pays to have reps spend time in the booth where they can gain more knowledge about your products and possibly make some valuable hometown contacts.

Content and format. In trying to develop an interesting and productive sales meeting, a sales manager for one of our principals sent us all a letter asking for our assistance in planning the event. He wanted to know what problems we were up against, which of his company's products should be featured, and any additional information that would help him make our two days most beneficial. Apparently, most of his reps put his request at the bottom of their correspondence file; several weeks later we received a second request for a reply.

When this reminder didn't bring a rush of ideas from his rep force, he tried a new tactic. Each rep was sent a third letter assigning him a subject on which he was to make a 30-minute presentation at the meeting. Since he had an active rapport with each rep and his territory, the sales manager was able to assign a good array of subjects. Aware of special situations that had arisen wherein the principal or the rep had come up with an innovative solution to a customer's problem, he asked each rep to explain how the right answer was developed. Now, instead of simply writing a brief letter outlining topics we thought would be of interest at the sales meeting, I and my fellow reps had to go to considerable lengths to talk to customers, get samples, and prepare a presentation.

Not only did it serve us right, but the end result was probably one of the best rep sales meetings I ever attended. Here were our counterparts from all over the country getting up and describing how they turned a problem into an order. The question and answer periods, usually dull, often lasted longer than the original presentation as the principal's other reps eagerly tried to discover how they could apply the same successful tactics with their customers. The sales manager and his associates had a hard time getting a word in edgewise, but they were obviously delighted at the interested response this new agenda had generated among their veteran reps.

Of course, all sales meetings should not be run by the reps; certain vital information about new products and policies can be conveyed only by company people. Normally the company must provide the leadership, planning, and agenda to assure a smooth, compact meeting full of meat and potatoes. But too often meetings are entirely one-sided, with all the information being provided by the principal. Without arrangements for a two-way communication session, the company loses a valuable opportunity to listen carefully to the field force. Reps can many times offer suggestions that will increase the company's success in the marketplace.

In contrast with the back-and-forth communication aimed at bringing mutual understanding of the problems facing the sales force and how they can be resolved, far more serious defects in a company's policies or practices often exist that reps won't comment on individually. They don't want to be singled out as troublemakers and prefer to remain silent rather than point out certain actions that may be seriously undermining their selling efforts. For this reason I believe you should have the courage to set aside an hour or two for a rep round-table session with no company people present.

While attending a meeting last year we were asked by the principal's sales manager to comment on a new commission structure the company contemplated putting into effect. This new structure would have benefited some reps and hurt others because of the product mix and the different types of customers to whom the products were sold. Present at the meeting—and eager to get an honest response—were several of the company's top officers. Very little comment was offered by the approximately 20 reps in attendance, none of whom was familiar with the circumstances of the others and with how they felt the commission change would affect them. I'm sure the management people were convinced they were dealing with a callous, unthoughtful group of reps; but had they been present at the heated discussions around the bar that evening, they'd have been astonished at the violent irritation stirred up by their proposals.

This situation could have been avoided if the company people had presented the proposed commission change and then strategically withdrawn from the room. Left alone, the reps would have done exactly what they did later that evening, but through an appointed spokesman they could have informed the management people of their concern about the suggested changes and detailed the reasons behind their feelings, thereby establishing a meaningful dialogue. The company officials wished neither to upset their reps nor to reduce their income, but by denying them the opportunity to discuss the matter privately, they created a poor atmosphere for the balance of the meeting.

A controversial proposal is not the only reason for a private rep round table. A gathering of this sort merely formalizes a lot of the informal talk that takes place over coffee or during late evening bull sessions. But instead of letting the steam dissipate merely as private conversation, company managers can benefit by collecting the thoughts of their reps on how the company can ameliorate problems that interfere with the success of their rep program.

Product information is always a necessary item of business at meetings; how well it's presented determines whether it's fully absorbed by your audience or passed off lightly. No matter how gifted the speaker, a lecture on a new product will never match a presentation that actually involves the meeting participants. Gatherings of three or four reps with an informed company man as leader are most effective, particularly if a show-and-tell procedure is practiced. If your product can be handled or operated by them, each rep can be drawn into the game by being permitted to get personally involved with the product in these small groups. This type of familiarity under the guidance of a knowledgeable instructor can do much to impart important product expertise—one of your reps' biggest assets when selling for you in the field.

Don't waste time making speeches on the basics of how to sell; each man has already developed a successful mode of selling or he wouldn't be able to support himself. But speeches on how to sell *your* product are a different story, provided they're presented by the sales manager or a leading rep who has successfully sold in the proposed manner.

All products have individual advantages which can result in an order over a competitive product if they're emphasized by the salesman. Often these advantages are not apparent, even to the rep, and remain unnoticed and unexploited simply because the obvious has not been presented to the sales force. At one sales meeting I attended, a rep gave a presentation on the good luck he had selling our principal's product by emphasizing only one of the product's several strong features. I had myself tended to stress all the features in my sales presentations with only fair success. By concentrating on an exciting feature that made the potential customer ask a question, the rep could quickly exploit the buyer's curiosity and expand on the other features of the item.

I couldn't believe such a simple approach would work, but I had nothing to lose by trying it. It worked exactly as the rep said it would, and my percentage of sales for that company has risen dramatically and most agreeably. As a bonus, it has made me more confident in my approach to prospective customers for that principal. I know I'll be able to arouse their interest almost immediately. The speaker who can talk from experience about how he sold the company's product can be a valuable part of your program.

I've always felt that a sales meeting is *not* the place for introducing a new product, particularly if it's of a technical nature. This is contrary to popular opinion in the sales community, where new products are often the reason sales meetings are held.

I'd like to suggest that new products be introduced several months prior to the date of your annual sales meeting, accompanied by a sufficient amount of promotion and descriptive literature. This allows your reps to get out into the field with the product, test it, feel it, and collect customers' reactions to it. The findings can then be profitably discussed among the reps and fed back to company personnel at the sales meeting. No matter how much testing has been performed, once a product is introduced there are always minor bugs and objections to be taken care of.

If your meeting is held after the reps have experienced some of the new product's quirks, both they and you will profit from the feedback and discussions that will naturally be a part of your meeting. On the other hand, when a product is introduced for the first time at a sales meeting, the reactions of the potential customers can't be anticipated and you'll have to come by these one by one at a later date, perhaps making costly trips to the territories and forfeiting the advantage of collective problem solving that a meeting can afford.

Presentations designed to be more policy- than product-oriented—for example, an explanation of the new five-year plan or management's forecast of the economic climate—are ideally presented at a luncheon or dinner interlude, or at the opening or closing of the meeting. If the meeting is held at a location near the home office, you can aid your communications program by inviting as many company people as possible to a refreshment hour and dinner: secretaries, switchboard operators, production people, anyone who remotely talks to or corresponds with your reps.

There's no substitute for meeting and talking with associates you've communicated with by phone or letter. It opens up a whole new area of awareness and friendliness between the reps and your personnel, and the extra cost is very small in relation to the large benefits that accrue from such a social event. My partner and I have noticed that after we've met and visited with personnel at our principals' plants, we seem to get a little extra service when we make a phone or letter request on behalf of our customers. Having attended these events when we worked as direct employees for a company several years ago, we know this extra socializing pays off on both ends.

A moment of truth. Your sales meeting should also provide for a moment of truth. By this I mean that at one point any anticipated problems should be stated candidly. Reps don't like bad news any more than anyone else, but they dislike being uninformed even more. Perhaps you know you're facing a strike, or a large unit used to make your best-selling item will require a two-month overhaul, drastically restricting production. These negative factors are unpleasant to contemplate and it's tempting to ignore them for fear of the reaction they'll stimulate.

However, by refusing to face the obvious, or worse still, by keeping your reps unaware of expected delays in your future plans, you'll create more problems than by being frank. Perhaps you're planning to discontinue a product, or change the appearance of another, or raise the price of your entire line. If you don't inform the rep of changes that he realizes were in progress at the time of the sales meeting, you deprive him of knowledge that can affect his relations and future business with important customers.

Of course, good reps also realize they can't be taken into confidence on all matters, but your candid briefings on subjects important to their selling strategy will be welcomed. On the other hand, if the rep returns to the field and shortly thereafter discovers that you've been less than open with him, particularly when such a good opportunity for openness was available, he'll begin to doubt all communications.

To neglect holding any form of sales meeting is a surefire way to fall behind your reps' other principals who do hold meetings. The company that uses every opportunity to upgrade its reps' knowledge of its product and its personnel scores high on the reps' attention scale, and thus receives more effort from the rep in return.

13

MANA

A helping hand to the manufacturer

What is now a strong alliance of manufacturers' representatives was not always so. In 1947 a group of pioneering individuals decided to attempt a loose coalition of practicing reps to protect their interests, advance the state of the art, and gain some collective advantages such as lowered insurance rates. Out of these initial objectives, the nonprofit organization called Manufacturers' Agents National Association (MANA) was formed. The organization was slow to attract reps on a national basis; most of its original members were from the West Coast.

From These Humble Beginnings

MANA limped along for many years. Its annual dues of $25, added to the lower group life and hospitalization insurance rates, made membership an intelligent and economic choice for many reps. But except for this isolated advantage, reps were offered little incentive to remain as members. No one had the time or inclination to investigate the variety of advantages a group of professional reps could generate for themselves and their principals. Over the years, because of this stagnation, many reps dropped their memberships.

The sixties brought about a rebirth of interest in the mutual needs of reps, many of whom had entered the field in the fifties and brought with them the experience they gained from their previous positions in industry. Many of these newer reps were dissatisfied with the lack of a firm MANA program that could speak strongly and fairly for their profession, not only to the manufacturing fraternity but also to the lawmakers in Washington where tax laws involving the small businessman can seriously affect his ability to survive and prosper.

Gradually, several of these more concerned reps took some calculated risks by spending their extra energies and resources to mold MANA into a viable organization that would realistically represent the field rep and give him a home base from which he could derive all the advantages he needed to make his agency a truly professional business. Because of the previous indifference of the leaders to the real needs of the reps and the resultant lack of interest on the part of the membership, this was going to prove to be a hard task. However, slowly but surely some of the veterans realized that a sincere drive was under way to bring them some of the things they had wanted when they joined MANA.

Perhaps the biggest breakthrough occurred in 1970 when Jim Gibbons completed the sale of his successful rep agency and—filled with enthusiasm because the agency business had been good to him—decided that he'd jump in with both feet and try to lead MANA to first-class status. He and the MANA officers, all well recognized as leaders in the rep business, knew that one of the best methods to gain recognition for the organization was to insist that it be conscious of the needs of the reps *and their principals*.

To emphasize this latter point during one of my visits to her office, Georgia Gibson, operations director of MANA and right-hand assistant to Jim Gibbons, told me: "MANA is not a union for representatives. We hope that some day we'll have as many principal firms as members as we do representatives." With about 4,400 members, of which 400 are associate members (principals), this is an ambitious and perhaps unrealistic goal, but it's an honest objective and it gives credence to MANA's recognition of the need for a well-balanced membership. By keeping itself posted on the views of firms employing reps, MANA's staff can make plans and decisions objectively.

A small firm just beginning a rep sales program can greatly increase its odds of succeeding by joining MANA as an associate member as early as possible. Not only will the firm immediately start receiving *Agency Sales,* the up-to-date monthly publication, but through MANA's reprint service it'll have free access to all the more noteworthy articles appearing there in the past.

Except for being unable to cast a vote or serve as an officer, associate members have the same rights as regular members. A small company unable to interest a local insurance firm in offering low group rates can thus provide good fringe benefits to its employees through enrollment in MANA's group insurance plans. Similar coverage for principals is extended to all MANA's other group plans, including an attractive car-leasing package contracted with one of the nation's leading car-leasing organizations. The savings accruing from these privileges can easily offset the modest dues of $65 a year and the one-time initiation fee of $25.

Associate members are able to request and receive aid from MANA's staff in disputes with their reps, and can count on a fair response. Its membership is interested in upholding MANA's professional status, and it views with displeasure all members who don't meet these high standards. Thus, when a rep isn't performing ethically or is simply not performing, MANA wants to know about it so it can make an intelligent suggestion to a principal that's asking for astute advice in resolving an unproductive situation.

Finding Who's Who and What's What

Among the specifically outlined benefits that can be expected by the members of MANA are a surprisingly large number that will accrue to the principal as well as the rep. Of particular importance are its publications.

Membership directory. Each year MANA publishes a directory listing all its members, and makes the publication available to nonmembers for a small fee. Companies searching for reps use this directory to ferret out MANA members for territories in which they wish to appoint reps. Until recently the members were listed by geographical area only, so that a sales manager using the directory had to analyze the lines of every rep in the targeted area to decide which reps sold a compatible product line.

In 1975 MANA changed all that by undertaking a massive reorganization of member data. The new version differs from previous issues the way the Yellow Pages of the phone book differ from the white pages—and then some. Associate members are listed first—a favored position. Each entry shows the company name, its address, its sales manager, and the products it wishes to list.

The main portion of the directory begins with an alphabetical listing of all rep members. Each entry includes the agency's name, its address, the person to contact, his telephone number, the agency's warehouse facilities if any, the number of salesmen, the territory they cover, the location of branch offices, the date the agency was established, and the year in which it became a member of MANA.

The second section of the directory is designed to cut down the time needed to find reps who have lines compatible with yours. Each product category includes the names of all agencies handling that type of product and the territories they serve. For example, if your company makes any type of rubber product, you can turn to the rubber-product listing and find every MANA member who chooses to be listed there. In this instance, you'll find 282 member agencies across the country currently selling rubber-related items. As you see, it's a rather complete product listing.

A complete listing of all agencies is again included in the third and last section, this time by territory and product lines. This section shows how many reps are selling products similar to yours in a given area. It also contains advertisements by reps who actively use this media for solicitation of new principals—the ads grouped according to territory location. Thus, by placing an ad in the directory, agencies are able to go beyond the conventional data shown in their listing and emphasize the types of lines they seek. Progressive reps also use these ads as image builders; some very attractive and informative ads are displayed in this section.

Aside from the copies sent free to members, the 1975 MANA directory was requested by approximately 25,000 individuals and companies. By far the majority of those purchasing a copy were companies that used it as a reference guide when searching for reps to sell their products.

Agency Sales. Timely articles on current problems in the rep field can help you understand some of the problems your reps face in the field. Reps, the editorial staff, and professional consultants contribute articles to this monthly publication, which is sent free to each member.

Agency Sales carries the usual articles on improving sales techniques, but the editorial staff chooses these wisely, recognizing that the readers are already professional sales people and articles that don't furnish something new or innovative in selling are not of interest. The bulk of the articles contain other helpful advice for the rep in conducting his business. There's a regular financial column covering everything from how to deal with your friendly IRS agent to how to set up a pension plan.

Attorneys commenting on contracts and other legal involvements are featured from time to time. Since the reps are essentially small businessmen, many of the points featured by these experts can also aid associate members whose size prohibits them from employing full-time financial and legal experts. Charley Hugg, a close friend and owner of the Clark Equipment Company franchise in Arkansas, recently asked me to send him reprints of a financial article he read in my copy of *Agency Sales* while visiting us with his family. Some of the articles are pertinent reprints from such trade journals as *Industrial Marketing* or *Sales Management,* publications the average rep reader may not receive.

Subjects are frequently directed to the principal. Many subscribers are sales managers whose firms are not necessarily associate members but who employ reps or are thinking about it. Aware of these readers as well as the associate members, the editor features articles by sales managers of companies using reps. The authors are encouraged to speak their mind on any aspect of their experiences, good or bad, that will help other principals and reps in their pursuit of more productive sales results.

As mentioned in an earlier chapter, the display and classified advertising departments are ideal meeting places for reps and principals with the same aim—a business association of mutual benefit.

Financial newsletter. A prominent CPA writes a monthly newsletter keeping the membership abreast of the latest developments in the financial and tax field. Since numerous rep agencies are corporations with many of the same problems as those incurred by principals, most of the material reported in this monthly advisory will interest you and your accounting department.

Also, again like some rep firms, many small companies using reps are sole proprietorships or partnerships, and since advice and information for these types of operations are common to both rep members and associate members, they're included in the publication whenever an important change is discovered in the tax laws.

Mel Daskal, the current author of the newsletter, is a rare breed—a CPA who has a way with words and possesses a devilish sense of humor. I read his comments for the fun of it, even if the subject isn't of particular interest to me.

Reprint service. Drawing on articles that appeared in *Agency Sales* and other prominent trade journals, MANA has collected a library of reprints that can be had for a modest charge of 25¢ each. (They are free to members.) Naturally, a good portion of these are of specific interest to rep members, but many were also written for the benefit of the principal. Here's a listing of those currently available that would be of interest to the manufacturer. (More are in the offing.)

How to Lay the Best Foundation for Sales Through Agents
Source of Manufacturers' Agents and Agency Salesmen
Is the Independent Sales Agent for You?
How to Build Volume with Representatives
How to Sell Successfully Through Manufacturers' Agents
How to Get Along with Sales Agents
Give Me the Sales Rep Any Day
The Case for Using Manufacturers' Representatives
Putting on Agents?
Should You Be Using a Manufacturers' Agent?
Understanding and Motivating the Manufacturers' Agent
How to Maintain the Balance Between Agent and Principal
Communications Is the Name of the Game
It's Time to Look at Your Agency-Manufacturer Agreement
Nine Things a Representative Owes to His Principal
How Should Agents Be Paid When Pioneering a New Product?
Survey of Commission Rates
How Do Manufacturers Work Out Split Commission Arrangements?
Know Your Contracts
Termination of Agency Contracts
MANA'S Marketing Guide

Information exchange. MANA isn't interested in adding associate members who'll use their membership as a front for unethical actions.

Some companies with poor track records in their relations with reps seek to add gloss to their reputations by joining MANA. To avoid adding such firms to the Association and to aid its members, MANA keeps a *Warn* file. This is a record, by company, of complaints received from member reps over the years about unfair practices perpetrated by principals they represented. These files contain criticisms relating to unreceived commissions, territorial disputes, undeserved terminations, and any other practices the complaining reps felt were not consistent with professional conduct.

The *Warn* file is edited with extreme caution, however, and a letter or two from a disgruntled rep doesn't result in an automatic downgrading of that company's reputation. Individual reps who consistently write complaining letters about unfair actions from their principals may be "protesting too much." It's when a company's file starts bulging with unfavorable reports that MANA takes a hard look at the reports and red-flags the company as a potential for serious offenses against the best interests of the membership, both reps and principals. MANA discourages membership applications from such firms.

Although keeping the membership of principals "clean" is a purpose of the *Warn* file, its main reason for existing is to help rep members avoid associating with principals that have poor reputations in dealings with their agents. No firm is ever blacklisted by MANA, but when a member requests information from the file about a prospective principal, he's referred to the very reps who lodged the original complaints.

The member is then free to consult with the offended reps and come to his own conclusion about representing the company in question. If the file contains only one or two complaints, the member will probably phone the complaining reps and perhaps discover that the offenses were minor or the rep was unfair in his appraisal. On the other hand, if MANA provides him with 10 or 15 references, he'll assume that the multitude of complaints speaks for itself.

The *Warn* file works two ways. On their part, associate members can inquire of the Association about the credentials of the various reps they're seeking to hire. Reps who have an unsavory history of unethical behavior are no more welcomed by MANA than companies with a similar notoriety. It's always best for an associate member to write for information on a prospective rep before offering him a contract. To do your part as a member, you should inform the Association of the unsatisfactory conduct of any rep, and so protect your fellow associate members from hiring the wrong man.

Regional seminars. Every several months a regional meeting is scheduled in one of the major metropolitan cities. These are geographically chosen over the years so that most members will find one held close enough to his location to enable him to attend conveniently. Members, associate members, and nonmembers are encouraged to participate in the activities. The seminar fee is modest, enough to cover expenses, although nonmembers are billed at a slightly higher rate.

These two-day affairs are not held for social purposes, but are truly shirt-sleeve sessions covering the gamut of rep operations. The only reason attendants agree to take time out for coffee breaks is to conduct individual discussions on the various subjects of personal interest.

The format provides for a variety of speakers, each covering a subject on which he's an expert. This isn't too far removed from the format of a normal seminar except for one glaring difference: participants are encouraged to interrupt the speaker at any point during his presentation if they have a question. It might seem that this would provoke considerable turmoil in the speaker's nervous system—like waiting for the other shoe to drop—but exactly the opposite occurs. The more the participants interrupt with questions, the more the speaker is caught up in the enthusiasm of the group.

I don't recall one programmed speaker getting through his entire speech without interruption during a seminar I attended in Houston. However, I do recall finding myself enthused over the amount of subjects covered and the variety of points discussed during the two-day session. In addition, the group broke up into smaller units for round-table discussions. Again the subjects were so interesting that the participants had difficulty choosing one discussion unit over the other, and some actually visited several before settling down.

Because of the wide range of products sold by reps there was seldom any problem involving competitive secrets; free-swinging participation was the rule rather than the exception. The star of one group—an exception—was a man who sold everything from bath towels to diesel engines, successfully. Being accustomed to selling products closely allied to each other, we were at a loss to figure out how he could accomplish such an unusual selling job—and he didn't tell us.

As a principal attending a MANA seminar, you'll find yourself in the real world of reps. I'm certain you'll come away impressed with the caliber of the men who pursue the vocation of the self-employed salesman. And who knows, maybe you'll discover a rep there to handle your line in a new territory.

A Stitch in Time . . .

While the foregoing features are indicative of the major advantages you can expect from your membership in MANA, there are a number of satellite aids and programs that add frosting to the cake.

Insurance plans. The Association has refined and is constantly reviewing its group insurance policies for the most coverage at the least cost consistent with good insurance practice. There's a plan for hospitalization and medical expenses, and additional group insurance policies offered include life insurance, disability insurance, accidental death and dismemberment insurance, and product and premises liabilities.

Commission arbitration. This service is invaluable for maintaining good relations between reps and their principals. Even though it may appear that contractual agreements cover the interpretation sufficiently, misunderstandings often arise in applying commission rates. A rep may have established an account in his area only to see the customer move to warmer climes and an agency in the new location reap the benefit of the rep's years of groundwork. Who's entitled to the commission? Should it be split? Should it be gradually adjusted in favor of the agency in the new area? Questions like these are important when a half-million-dollar account is at stake. Because of the variety of such situations that can occur, defining who gets the commission and how much is almost impossible to cover in the rep-principal contract.

In cases like this the MANA staff brings into play its arbitration counseling service and asks each party for its version of the circumstances surrounding the controversy. After analyzing both sides of the question and drawing on their years of experience in arbitrating just such occurrences, the staff will make a recommendation to both parties for the amicable settlement of the problem.

The recommendation isn't binding on either party. A strong attempt is made to recommend a plan of action that'll keep the two parties on a friendly business relationship. This is really the heart of the counseling service. If only the distribution of commissions is in question—and not the good faith of either party—an effective team sales effort has probably taken place. MANA goes to great lengths to insure a continuation of such a relationship since it means good business for both the rep and the principal.

Of course there are firms that choose to take unfair advantage of their reps in one form or another, including peculiar interpretations of contractual agreements or simply nonpayment of commissions. Here, when the abuse is flagrant, the MANA staff points out that if the company expects to continue marketing its wares through professional reps, it must treat its current reps in a professional manner. Failure to conduct an ethical rep program can only reflect badly on the reputation of the company within rep circles and make it more difficult for the firm to hire competent agencies to work for it in the future. Attesting to the effectiveness of this service is the collection of over $500,000 in commissions for member agencies in the past five years.

The majority of companies using reps adhere to high moral standards, and most counseling services are called into play in cases of misunderstanding regarding the paying of commissions rather than in cases of intentional abuse of rep-principal relationships. Having an impartial body familiar with the nature of these misunderstandings can help hold together a profitable relationship that might falter without the insight MANA can provide.

List of attorneys and accountants. Since reps have been forced to become more sophisticated in financial and legal matters because of the encroaching mass of government red tape and regulation faced by all business concerns, they've had to find skilled professionals to guide them through the morass. The unusual nature of their business, however, makes the search more than commonly frustrating.

Although your friendly neighborhood barrister would have you believe otherwise, few attorneys understand the rep business. This means fees are somewhat higher for a rep seeking help in interpreting a principal's contract or taking legal action to recover commissions due him, because the rep is paying for the lawyer's time while he's learning what the rep business is all about. And to a lesser degree this is also true of CPAs. Their function is somewhat more consistent, but a few among this august group will still stare at you blankly when you tell them you're a manufacturers' representative.

Over the past few years, however, we've discovered certain of these gentlemen in both professions who have become skilled in handling the affairs of reps. Recognizing the difficulty its members have in identifying these experts merely by the sign on their door or their listing in the Yellow Pages, MANA has encouraged us to submit the names and addresses of those who we've found to be particularly effective in dealings with us. Aside from including a ringer or two who may have been recommended by a brother-in-law rep, MANA has compiled an excellent listing of attorneys and accountants recommended by fellow members across the country. The list is periodically updated as new names are submitted.

How can this help you? Well, you face the same problem as your reps, especially if you're a smaller firm with a handful of reps in the field. You require the assistance of an attorney in drawing up your rep contracts and in other matters concerning the legal and tax implications of marketing through reps. An accountant or CPA familiar with the rep business can also help you in costing and budgeting for a rep program.

As an associate member privy to the MANA listing of recommended attorneys and accountants, you should be able to find someone on the list within shouting distance of your office. Employing an expert on reps in either field not only can save you money in fees but will result in more professionalism in the advice you pay for and receive.

Contracts. MANA is not in the business of practicing law, but it has gone to considerable expense in developing sample legal agreements that can be referred to by your attorneys when they draw up a standard contract to be used by your company with its reps.

The *Standard Form of Agreement* between agent and manufacturer covers eight pages and outlines almost every detail that could arise in the rep-principal relationship. It covers territory and customers; terms and length of contract; pricing and terms of purchase, handling, and acceptance of orders; terms of commissions on orders; supplies and deliveries; invoices and collections; selling aids, literature, and promotion; training; availability of information; improvement in services; product warranty; handling of inquiries; shipment reports; selling effort; relationship created; hold harmless clause; termination; notices and requests; controlling agreement; assignment; and adjustment and adjudication of disputes.

This agreement is for the rep or principal who wants to be protected under every conceivable condition that could arise. Your legal fees should be fairly modest if your lawyer uses this agreement as a guide in formulating your rep contract. Aside from making a few additions that may be needed for your particular type of company or product, he'll be able to edit this agreement quickly into a legal document that would make any lawyer beam with pride.

The MANA agreement was not dreamed up overnight. Over the years, as new circumstances arose and legal adjustments were made in rep-principal lawsuits, MANA's lawyers revised the agreement to cover those circumstances. These changes were always made in the interests of eliminating the causes of misunderstandings that themselves led to the disagreements that prompted legal action. MANA's philosophy is to allow as much room as possible for mutual understanding and negotiation in any situation that could lead to disagreements, thereby reducing the number of disputes that ultimately wind up in the courts.

The form is free to members, but I again emphasize that its purpose is to serve as a guide for your attorney rather than as a complete contract in itself. For those reps or principals who are not interested in a lengthy contract but do want to cover the essentials, a *Short Form Agency Agreement* is available. This is a one-page sample which highlights the important considerations in a rep-principal contract: sales policies, orders and collections, agent's commissions, relationship created, term or length of contract, hold harmless clause, and notices. This form also serves only as a guide.

For its rep members, MANA has drawn up two additional sample contracts: a *Trade Secrecy and Noncompetition Agreement* and a *Purchase and Sale Agreement*. The latter is an eight-page form for reps who are merging with, buying, or selling an agency. Certain elements of both contracts could be of assistance to small firms under certain conditions.

Auto-leasing program. If your company has only a few leased cars, you'll certainly benefit by using the plan MANA has negotiated with a major auto-leasing company. The automobile is of vital importance to every rep; every member is therefore a potential user of the lease plan. This widespread need has made it possible for MANA to obtain an excellent rate structure, as many reps will attest. Unless yours is an exceptionally large organization, you'll almost certainly be unable to match the scope and cost of the program offered to the members and associate members of MANA.

Auto rental discount. Again, because of the size of the MANA membership and the potential it offers for short-term auto rentals, a 20 percent discount is available to you and your company at one of the country's largest auto rental agencies with offices wherever cars are rented: airports, hotels, motels, and resort areas.

A Code of Ethics

In this chapter I've given several examples of why individual services offered by MANA are worth far more than the modest dues required to be an associate member. But of more importance to you and your reps are the additional benefits that accrue as a result of the support your firm and other companies give the MANA organization. By support I don't mean only financial support. An active associate membership can do much to influence the future direction of MANA and to bring about a closer and more intimate and trusting relationship between reps and their principals.

With the help of its total membership, the MANA organization has drawn up the code of ethics reprinted here. As more principals join MANA and conscientiously follow the intent of the code, both reps and principals can reduce the number of misunderstandings and disagreements and set about meeting the objective of their relationships— selling the product!

CODE OF ETHICS

1. TO BE ACCORDED THE MANUFACTURER BY THE AGENT:
☐ Comply with established policies of the manufacturer.
☐ Conscientiously cover the territory assigned.
☐ Avoid misrepresentation in any form or manner.
☐ Restrict lines or accounts with principals to those which can well be handled.
☐ Give the manufacturer the same loyal service as the agent, operating his own business, expects from his own employees.

2. TO BE ACCORDED THE AGENT BY THE MANUFACTURER:

☐ Enter into a fair and clearly worded agreement with the Manufacturers' Agent.

☐ Make the agreement cancellable by either party during its first year on suitable advanced written notice, but subsequently only for failure of either party to comply with its terms, or by mutual consent.

☐ Refrain from any modification whatever of the terms of such agreement, except by mutual consent after full and friendly discussion of the reasons for such desired modification.

☐ Extend to the Manufacturers' Agent the same benefits available to the manufacturer's own salaried employees, wherever possible.

☐ Refrain from absorbing, refusing, or cutting the Manufacturers' Agent's established commissions for any reason whatever.

☐ Provide practical and dignified means for friendly arbitration of all controversial points that may arise between agent and principal.

3. TO BE ACCORDED ONE MANUFACTURERS' AGENT BY ANOTHER:

☐ Exchange trade information, in the mutual interest.

☐ Avoid any suggestion or agreement to divide commissions with those representing other than the agent's own principals.

☐ Refrain from soliciting from manufacturers the known lines or accounts of other established Manufacturers' Agents by unfair methods.

☐ Cooperate to upbuild the profession of the Manufacturers' Agent—by supporting the National Association established for that purpose, subscribing to its aims and objectives, and in every practical way working to advance the interests of all Manufacturers' Agents and Representatives.

14

PUTTING IT ALL TOGETHER

And now it's up to you!

There's no shortcut to success in the management of manufacturers' sales representatives. It requires a degree of diligence that's underestimated by the majority of firms wishing to use this form of marketing. On the surface it appears deceptively simple: no employment agency fees, no extensive interviews, no salaries, no fringe benefits, no supervision. It seems like a sales manager's dream come true—these are precisely the obligations that bog him down in his attempts to get into the field where the action is. The rep route also appeals to management people, particularly those in smaller firms where a direct regional or national sales program is impossible for lack of capital.

The Wise Sales Manager Proceeds Cautiously

But while it's an ideal method for accomplishing that result, its obvious simplicity is a trap for the unwary. Instead of studying and recognizing the differences between a casually administered program and a strategically planned program, most firms take the easy approach. And it appears to work—initially.

It's no problem to line up a group of reps to sell a company's product. Place a few advertisements in the right publications and it isn't even necessary to leave the office. Interviews and appointments can be handled by phone and mail, and within a few weeks the sales manager can hang a map of the United States on the wall and pin multicolored flags in the major marketing areas, confident that he has or will soon have bona fide reps established in each area.

From that point on, however, the program usually heads straight downhill. One or two of his choices may turn out to be winners, but his performance will suffer badly in comparison with that of the sales manager who launches a program with the expertise needed to hire and motivate a select group of professional representatives.

Such a sales manager will have first made a complete analysis of his organization to determine its ability to adjust to and support a true rep program. His appraisal will include a nonillusionary assessment of the company's top personnel, including the owner or president. It's useless to begin recruiting if the top men are blocking effective administration of a dynamic program. A stubborn production manager or an erratic owner could doom a program before it got started.

The wise sales manager will proceed only if he's convinced that his company is suited to the rep way of selling, or that with proper indoctrination the obvious drawbacks can be eliminated or at least reduced to practical levels. He'll have completely planned his campaign before taking his first step, and he'll outline his program to his top management and receive their complete backing. He'll start slowly, choosing his areas carefully, and he'll explore all possible avenues of reaching the professionals in those territories.

Not content with placing one ad in a trade journal, he'll investigate other routes to gaining the attention of the best reps available. After analyzing the responses and discarding all but the most promising, he'll visit the area and conduct extensive interviews with the candidates. He'll avoid making an impulsive decision, and he may even have two or three interviews with the finalists to insure that his choice is the best possible.

He'll have prepared a fair and reasonable contract, in plain language, outlining the company's policies in the company-rep relationship, and he'll make sure that both the company's and the rep's obligations are plainly stated. In the first rush of heady anticipation, he'll successfully resist the temptation to award territories larger than his instinct and research tell him he should, despite the promises of massive orders that less responsible reps will make. Except for the territory clause, his contract will be consistent for all his reps, and conditions will not change for any one rep regardless of that individual's demands for special considerations as a condition of signing the contract.

The sales manager will not recruit the reps in one fell swoop, realizing that by thus diluting his energies in trying to administer a meaningful program practically overnight, he may place the whole effort in jeopardy. As he gradually appoints reps throughout his marketing area, he'll become aware of the wisdom of a slow but steady recruitment campaign. His early appointments may not show the promise he expected; he may have made some errors in choosing his group because of inexperience or overeagerness; but his later choices will benefit from these oversights and miscalculations.

He'll also begin to recognize that the subtle and exacting job of hiring reps is perhaps the easiest part of his entire program, for the proof of his excellence lies in results—orders, to be exact. In taking on the difficult task of motivating his rep group, he'll immediately recognize that he's no longer able to act alone. Only with the complete cooperation of his entire organization can he hope to achieve the results in the field that were the basic stimulus for launching his ambitious marketing strategy.

From the beginning he must be able to guarantee a smooth flow of information designed to keep his reps and inside personnel constantly aware of the status of pending orders and all the other small details that give a customer the impression that a company knows what it's doing. Anything less creates confusion, not only among the customers but among the reps as well. This is no doubt the toughest hurdle the sales manager will have to overcome. People are naturally more concerned with their own daily duties, and bringing them to a new and acute awareness of the need for good communications with the company's reps is a challenge that requires constant attention.

The sales manager's next responsibility is to convince his people of the importance of maintaining a competitive pricing structure, consistent high quality in the product being marketed, and on-time shipments of promised goods. A breakdown in any of these three highly visible obligations will show the company's rep force gradually losing interest in the daily battle to gain orders for the company's product.

The sales manager must have his management's commitment to a creative advertising and sales promotion program. His reps need all the help they can get, particularly if his competitors excel in providing their own reps with this vital assistance. A pretty brochure doesn't guarantee orders for your reps, but the more familiar his principal's name is to prospective buyers the more chance he has for success; such recognition opens doors that may be tightly shut or only slightly ajar.

The company must also be ready and willing to provide field service for the reps when it's needed. This responsiveness convinces both the rep and his customer of the seriousness of the firm's intent to provide well-rounded support, thereby solidifying the impression of a company concerned with the customer's order from its receipt by the rep to the successful use of the product.

Realizing that routine reports from his reps are practically unobtainable, the sales manager will call for information from the field only when he can convince his reps that their compliance will ultimately be in their own best interest. Reports and forecasts must have a meaning that's apparent, and even then the sales manager will have to coax and cajole his reps to receive such information on time. Their reluctance to comply stems more from lack of time than from any desire to ignore these requests. Quotas are a notoriously poor method of increasing rep sales, and the sales manager will use other techniques to heighten incentives. Most of these will involve higher commissions of one sort or another.

He'll plan regular sales meetings for his reps and see to it that they're conveniently timed for the best attendance possible. A full-participation meeting will be planned that will not include dreary and useless exhortations by paid professional sales consultants; rather, every attempt will be made to get the rep's point of view on company policies and performance as these relate to the reps' efforts in the field. The sales manager, his staff, and company executives will take seriously all comments offered by their reps and will seek to correct whatever shortcomings are pointed out.

Finally, the sales manager will be cognizant of the advantages offered by the professional agencies serving the rep field, the most prominent of which is MANA. By subscribing to MANA's publications, or even having his company join as an associate member, he'll receive current information about new theories, new legislation, and the latest practices pertinent to the effective administration of a rep sales program.

The Successful Sales Manager Is Believable

Although the techniques outlined in each chapter of this book lay the groundwork for a vigorous and successful rep program, the real secret of making it work is development of a *believability profile* with your reps. A company whose actions—not words—can convince its rep field force that it has a sincere wish to develop and maintain a successful rep program will usually wind up with the brass ring.

There's no quick way to reach such a status with current or new reps. An occasional variance or mistake will occur; this is natural. But as a mountain climber must crisscross the terrain to reach the summit, you may have to use a diversity of apparently divergent means to reach your goal. However, if it's obvious that, despite these errors and setbacks, the direction of your program is toward a truly effective support plan for your reps, you'll gradually win their loyalty. This may take six months or six years, but when your company finally establishes a *believability profile* it will be recognized as a professional rep-oriented organization, and this will open more and more doors for it among the reps it needs to refine its sales efforts.

Few of our agency's principals follow the complete range of recommendations outlined in the preceding chapters, yet most project an image of *believability* to us through the day-to-day conduct of their business. The way they answer our questions, support us in the field, aid our (their) customers, keep us informed, and react to the multitude of information transactions required gradually builds in our mind the image of the company's dedication to the rep mode of selling. This policy has to be set by top management people, and they must convey to all company personnel that the rep group is to receive the same attention and treatment as direct employees of the firm are shown.

In almost all those cases where I've observed that management people have looked on their reps as valuable assets of the firm rather than as commissioned independents, that attitude has prevailed throughout the entire firm. This diffusion of your positive attitude is essential if the reps are to gain an overall impression of your willingness to back up their daily selling efforts. While this should stop considerably short of religious fervor, it nevertheless is important to a rep's selling drive that he believe what he's saying to the customer about the principals he represents.

The same quality that reps are looking for in their principals should govern your appraisal of prospective and current reps. The relationships we've tried to promote in these chapters are two-way streets, and your reps should show the same desire to become a part of your organization as you show to enlist them in your cause.

As pointed out, many hiring and motivating procedures that are indigenous to a direct sales force will not work with a rep force; but many other procedures are also available that will work with that group if the individuals in it react to those procedures satisfactorily. One occasionally finds reps who take on lines for the commissions the territory is already producing or who habitually seek to steal other reps' lines by promises of larger volume—they do indeed exist in every marketplace. And there are some reps who are just plain lazy. However, there's no excuse for keeping those reps who don't return your efforts in kind. You can follow the suggestions in this book to the letter, but with several unresponsive reps in your stable, your attempts to use a rep sales force to sell your products won't be successful.

By becoming known for the success of your rep program, you'll have more of the professionals competing for your line. With proper planning you can hire these professionals, whose performance will stand out vividly against that of reps of lesser caliber. If your reputation is poor, of course, then candidates will come in fewer numbers, and with less to choose from your chances of hiring truly effective professionals become noticeably slimmer.

If you're just beginning your program you do have a positive factor working for you: having started on the right path, you can continue on it. Even though you'll experience your share of errors and progress will be slow at first, you'll have an advantage over a competitor who has committed numerous careless mistakes in administering his rep sales program over the years. Despite his honest attempts to correct it, his poor reputation will be hard to overcome. Legends die hard, and the longer he has directed his field force badly, the longer it will take him to gain the credence needed to begin attracting the men who can bring his sales up to expectations.

The man with the most to gain in the shortest time is the sales manager or owner who has established *believability* with his reps but who still comes up short in the results department because he fails to understand all the requirements he must meet to achieve his true potential. He may have a good reputation and a sincere ambition to improve an already moderately successful rep sales program without knowing how to accomplish this. By reviewing the suggestions and observations I've outlined, he may be able to spot a sensitive communications area that's been neglected, or may find that his interviewing tactics turn off the very reps he'd like most to hire. Now that he understands the characteristics of the rep's personality or appreciates the importance of enlightened communication, perhaps one or two changes will make all the difference in the world on the sales chart.

Whether you're new to this age-old marketing method or a veteran seeking to improve results, your reps want you to succeed. Their success is limited only by your capabilities and ambitions. A strong, intelligent, sincere dedication to all the principles involved in motivating your professional manufacturers' representatives will lead to a productive and profitable sales future for your company.

15

THOUGHTS ALONG THE HIGHWAY

While compiling the strategies that lead to a successful rep sales program, I came upon a number of ideas and observations—some admittedly unorthodox—that could find no proper place within the scope of the individual chapters. I've assembled these in an informal grouping of no specific sequential order. If you absorb these reflections in the same spirit in which they're offered, you may find yourself occasionally departing from conventional sales management techniques, and the exploration of this new terrain could make your rep program a bit more exciting and a lot more profitable.

Timing Is Important

During recessions, it's common for our incoming mail to increase in volume. Unfortunately, this increase doesn't consist of orders but, instead, of rather desperate inquiries from companies seeking representation in our marketing areas.

Our own strategy in lean economic times is to double our efforts on behalf of our tried and true principals—those whose pricing, quality, and service have been dependable year in and year out. Our resources are limited, so to try to introduce a new line when the business cycle is at a low ebb is costly. We're familiar with the products of our present companies, and our calls on their behalf are a common-sense route to self-preservation when buyers are reducing their purchasing requirements.

The classified pages of prominent business publications will also abound in *Manufacturers' Representatives Wanted* ads. Many of these are placed by companies normally heavily committed to industries feeling the economic pinch the worst. Most representatives and buyers are well aware of these temporary diversification efforts, and neither group is anxious to abandon companies that have performed well in the past in return for some short-lived price advantage that will disappear when the economy regains its healthy state.

On the other hand, if your company has overemphasized its dependence on one industry and sincerely wishes to diversify its customer list, then hoard your resources during the recession and prepare for future marketing moves. As the economic climate warms up and buyers begin purchasing for inventory, they'll look more seriously at firms that make a concerted attempt to penetrate a market with every intention of staying there. And as buyers show a willingness to explore the merits of new vendors, reputable reps will be more receptive to taking on and introducing new lines.

Spending your rep-search budget as the economy improves will be wiser and more profitable than frantically using these funds to recruit a force during slow economic periods. As you gradually build your rep group, you'll be readying a seasoned and enthusiastic team that should be able to ease the pain of future slowdowns.

Want Inflation-Proof Salesmen?

There's no question that the cost of sales will rise at a faster rate than many of your company's other expenses. Contributing to this acceleration is the skyrocketing cost of travel. Travel is essential: your salesmen must see your customers or you'll lose them to firms whose sales people make frequent calls. Also rising are the costs of lodging, meals, and entertainment.

So your boss will probably call you in and point out that sales costs have risen from 4 or 5 percent to 7 or 8 percent of gross sales. You'll be told to cut back and get costs in line. This may mean holding the line on salaries, a move not calculated to improve the humor of your hardworking salesmen—and needless to add, an unhappy salesman is not inclined to sprint out of the office Monday morning head held high and eyes bright with enthusiasm. He's more likely to grouse with fellow salesmen down at the local coffeehouse for an hour or two. So you're caught between two forces and sales productivity suffers—which further lowers your frustration threshold.

Now consider the contrast to this offered by a rep program. Your percentage of sales costs stays the same. In our industry the commission rate of 5 percent has not changed within my memory. True, our dollar income has risen as the price of our principals' products has risen, but the *percentage* of sales costs to total selling price remains the same.

By selling through reps you maintain a fixed sales cost percentage and the shoe is on the other foot. Now it's management's obligation to hold down the total cost of the product in order not to increase the dollar cost of sales. That's just one less worry you have, which probably brings your total weekly worries down to about 78.

Form Letters Seldom Work

After purchasing the MANA directory, some companies apparently figure enough money has been spent on seeking reps. A general letter is composed telling about the firm's interest in finding a rep; the old mimeograph is cranked up to minimize further expense; and 30 or 40 copies of the letter are printed. These are handed to a secretary who's instructed to fill in names and addresses of reps listed in the MANA directory, and they're mailed to reps in the area where the firm would like to establish representation.

Our agency receives a number of letters every month asking about our interest in representing different firms. About 40 percent of them are form letters. We react to them much as the sender would if he were to receive a similar letter from a rep seeking his line. We ignore them. All others receive a reply.

Through our association with fellow reps we find that their philosophy is much the same. The sender of a form letter implies that he's too busy to take the time necessary to conduct a personal search and is using the most expedient method available to generate replies. What he may not realize is that his attitude reflects his administrative abilities and that no rep wishes to become associated with a sales manager who's insensitive to the need for a personal approach to communication.

Form letters are a necessary part of business and perform many useful functions when routine announcements are necessary, but avoid their use when recruiting reps. Ten personal letters will pull more legitimate replies than 50 form letters will.

Fish or Fowl?

It's not unusual for firms with a nationwide rep force to handle sales in their regional market with direct men; usually these are the sales manager and one or two sales people. However, for every firm selling in this manner, there's one that uses reps exclusively, even in its own backyard. Either course seems to work, but the firms having the most trouble with their sales programs are those that follow no consistent pattern, using both reps and direct men indiscriminately throughout the country.

Administering direct salesmen contrasts strikingly with administering a rep force. Salaries versus commissions, expenses versus no expenses, directives instead of suggestions—all these differences tax the flexibility of a communications program and introduce inefficiencies into the system. One of the prime goals of the mix-and-match approach is to rigidly control sales costs by placing direct men in the most desirable and profitable markets and reps in the fringe areas. It won't work—anyway, not effectively.

A rep likes to think of his market as viable for each of his principals and for the realization of each company's objective. To replace him with a direct man if the volume increases to the point where it becomes economically feasible to do so may lead him to create just enough sales to keep commissions below the amount needed for a changeover. Or, knowing that productive results mean the end of the line for him, he may be led to pay little attention to selling the principal's product.

Early in the game, make your decision to go one way or the other and try to stick with it. Consistency in administering your sales program helps everybody do a better job of selling.

Goodbye Old 80/20

The old rule is finally starting to fade away. As long as I can remember, prominent business executives have been intoning with ritualistic fervor that 80 percent of their business is done with 20 percent of their customers. I could never decide whether they looked on this with favor or disfavor, but at least they were consistent with their figures and enjoyed quoting them.

The tired old cliché was repeated again by a prominent sales executive in a recent issue of a sales trade journal. However, in an unrelated article in that same issue a manufacturing executive was quoted as saying that any company that has to rely on the 80/20 formula is neglecting a goodly portion of potential business.

By the same token it's been popularly noted that 80 percent of the business received by a company is brought in by 20 percent of the sales force. This is even more ludicrous than the first statement. If it were true, companies could drastically reduce the size of their sales force, since, according to this philosophy, only 20 percent of the salesmen were effective.

It's apparent that the 80/20 rule did apply at one time to many businesses that sold their goods to large retailers such as Sears, Roebuck or Montgomery Ward, and there are isolated instances of the 80/20 ratio even today; but if your rep group is performing in such a lopsided fashion, then something's wrong, either with the caliber of your reps, the selling philosophy of your company, or possibly your company's satisfaction with the status quo.

Regardless of your reasons for staying with it, it's a very vulnerable position in today's fast-changing, competitive environment. And having most of your business depend on the needs of a few customers or the talents of one or two reps is a dangerous pursuit.

Cost of Average Sales Call—Does it Matter?

A popular pastime among business prognosticators is to compute the cost of the average sales call and to show how the cost of each call steadily rises as the years go by. In almost any trade journal you'll find some authority stating that the present sales call now averages $65 or $75 (or set your own figure). Most often this figure is estimated by an executive of a firm selling some product or service designed to reduce the cost of these calls. It may be quoted by a representative of the telephone company, a compact-car manufacturer, or an airline company.

We all know that the costs of sales calls are rising, perhaps faster than general economic costs, because so many costs related to sales visits are expensive to begin with: meals, cars, gasoline, and air fares. But the cost of calls is not of first importance to the company using manufacturers' representatives; these companies pay for results, not for sales calls.

While calling on a customer one day, I waited in the reception room along with a direct man employed by a major adhesive firm. As salesmen do, we chatted, and I discovered that his company required him to make 12 calls a day, 5 days a week, or 60 calls every week. He soon glanced at his watch and said, "My 15 minutes are up," indicating that this was as long as he could afford to wait for any one buyer and still squeeze in his 12 calls for the day. His company could easily estimate the cost of each call by dividing his weekly salary and upkeep by 60. Determining the effectiveness of his calls, however, would be almost impossible.

I'm sure a company with such stringent rules would never be able to adjust to the rep style of selling where calls are made for results, not numbers. I've waited literally hours when I was relatively certain the wait would be worth it. I've also left my card and departed when a buyer could not see me promptly, using my own judgment as to the merits of my decision.

If your company is hung up on the quantity but not necessarily the quality of its salesmen's calls, stay with direct men. That way you'll be able to correctly estimate the cost of each sales call. Knowing exactly how much each call is costing them will make statistics-minded managers happy: the only shock they'll receive is when they analyze the amount of sales volume received per call made.

Are You Acquisition-Minded?

Companies wishing to diversify or grow through the acquisition of other companies pay a finder's fee to organizations that specialize in locating prospective candidates for acquisition. These specialists do a good job of seeking out the type of company whose goals are compatible with the client company's goals, and they're constantly in touch with company managements that wish to be acquired for one reason or another.

However, if your company is interested in acquiring another firm but is a beginner in the game, among the firms trotted out for your inspection you may find a number that have been reviewed and rejected many times by more sophisticated and experienced conglomerate organizations. These giants have the ability and know-how to recognize a pig in a poke, whereas your lack of experience may cause you to miss some of the major, but hidden, defects in a prospective candidate.

Think of your rep group as another source of information about heretofore unknown and unpublicized companies that may be interested in selling their business to you. Reps have a wide range of acquaintances in the business fraternity and are often on a first-name basis with several small-business owners. Your reps may have been selling to these firms for years and may have a real feel for the capabilities of the personnel and a deep insight into the reasons for the successes and failures of the company's marketing and production efforts. Some reps are so well acquainted with their customers' potential that it's not unusual for a rep to purchase a firm himself. I know several who own firms they've bought.

If you're serious about growing in this manner, alert your reps to your wish and set out some guidelines describing the type of acquisition you're seeking: the size, the general type of product, the location, and any other requirements that will help in identifying logical candidates. But don't initiate a program in this way with the idea of saving the finder's fee. Without this reward included as an incentive, your results will be about the same as they'd be if you asked the reps to sell your products without a commission.

Do Your Rep (and Yourself) a Favor

If you're a good, conscientious sales manager with faith in your rep group, you doubtless picture your loyal troops out selling your product day in and day out. It's comforting to envision 10 or 12 reps knocking on doors Monday through Friday enthusiastically promoting the sale of your company's widgits or wagon wheels.

In reality, in a given week, a rep may make a number of calls selling another principal's widgits. These are different from yours or he wouldn't be selling them. They're probably larger or smaller, but in either case they're complementary to your company's product, not competitive. He may make a call on a customer who doesn't buy your type of widget, but he hopes to sell one of his other principals' widgets.

Then suddenly, to his surprise, the customer has stopped buying larger and smaller widgets and is now buying the size you manufacture. The rep promptly solicits business for your firm. Great! Although the makers of the larger and smaller widgets are out of luck on this call, your company may realize a sale. However, if your rep hadn't handled the other two principals' lines he may not have made that particular call, in which case all three principals would have lost out, as well as the rep.

This is a roundabout way of making a point, but a similar loss can occur when you reply to an unsolicited inquiry from a firm whose requirement you can't fill because the item is too big, too small, or generally unsuited to your type of manufacture. Normal procedure is to reply, regretfully informing the purchasing agent that you're sorry you can't supply his part.

A copy of your letter—perhaps perfunctory and devoid of details—is sent to the rep, who may well have a principal who can easily make the item. But since in most cases the rep can't tell from your letter what the item is, a chance for a possible sale falls by the wayside. In this example you've lost nothing, but the rep may have lost a commission and one of his other companies may have missed an opportunity for a sale. Suppose, however, that your firm was one of those other companies.

One of the basic advantages of the rep style of selling is the crossbreeding effect that benefits *all* the companies represented by a good commissioned man. I've detailed a number of instances where this has paid off handsomely. Recommendation: Whenever you have to decline to quote on any item that might even remotely be handled by one of your reps, do the following:

1. Send the rep a copy of the inquirer's letter, blueprints, samples, and so on. Ask him to reply directly, advising the company of your inability to help it.
2. Insist that the rep provide you with a copy of his letter or a report on his call to guarantee that he has followed through.

By being allowed to make this contact, your rep may be able to capitalize on the original inquiry by selling the firm one of his other lines; or perhaps some other item it buys may be made by your company. By insisting on feedback from the rep you assure yourself that the inquiry has been answered. If you don't receive timely replies from him, discontinue the practice, since your company should make certain that all inquiries are answered in one form or another.

Giving him an opportunity to make a purposeful call is always more productive for a rep than his making a cold call or no call at all—there's always the possibility that some worthwhile business will result.

How Valuable Is a New Customer?

Is he valuable enough to warrant paying a few percentage points more in commissions on the first order or for the first year? New customers are the lifeblood of any growing organization, since old customers may go out of business, be the victims of a take-over, or find new local suppliers with lower prices. Most progressive firms place an almost obsessive emphasis on developing new accounts. We receive a monthly bulletin from one principal describing its new accounts, what they make, how each account was sold, and their future potential. This helps us and other reps to discover and service similar companies in our areas.

But a new account is hard to come by. All reps have regular customers who have learned to depend on the rep's service and the quality of his principals' products, but like any growth organization the rep must continue to add new customers to his portfolio. Finding and servicing new customers costs a firm more money than merely servicing a current customer, and the same applies for the rep. He has to make more calls without results—popularly or unpopularly known as missionary work—to identify the occasional prospect that warrants further solicitation. He may then call on the company for months or years before obtaining an order.

I haven't had any personal experience with firms that offer the incentive of temporarily higher commissions as a reward for finding a new customer, but I think it would pay dividends if it were tried. Your reps would appreciate your understanding of the difficult route they face in coming up with new customers, and awarding them a higher commission might spark an extra effort.

Since the first order is usually on a trial basis and is often not large, the increased commission may have a stronger stimulus if paid on all orders received within a year of establishing the new account. This could mean a few extra dollars in bookkeeping costs—but how much is a new customer worth? Just the future of your business, that's all!

Design Your Brochures with the Rep in Mind

A chief complaint of sales reps concerns the brochures and other literature provided them by their principals: they invariably fail to provide a specially designed location for the rep's agency's imprint. Sales promotion and advertising experts who create promotional pieces seldom consider the inevitable rubber-stamp imprint used by reps on each brochure to indicate that they represent the company in their marketing territory. The principal's name is usually prominently displayed on the front and back covers of a typical brochure, but the rep often has difficulty finding a spot to squeeze in his own name and address. This makes an otherwise well-prepared promotional piece look like the work of amateurs.

With a little planning, a good commercial artist or printer can easily design a small white space on the cover that will serve as an ideal spot for the rep's imprint. Strategically placed, this space will not take away from the attractiveness of the brochure, which can also be used by direct company sales people without the imprint. For a few extra dollars you can even have this space imprinted with the rep's name and address before supplying the brochures to your rep force; then you'll have a professional-appearing piece of literature, unsullied by rubber stamps.

How to Make a Friend for Life

Try the retainer method. "But that's against the basic principle of a rep program," you argue. "The reason reps are hired is to eliminate early start-up costs in a territory. The rep costs us nothing until he produces some sales."

Believe it or not, we were put on a retainer of $600 a month for approximately six months by a company that had some business in our area but was seeking more. The retainer was instituted about two years after we started our agency and was of tremendous help in keeping us afloat. Imagine our feelings toward a firm that took our fledgling agency and showed its confidence in our determination and ability by sending us $600 a month and saying, "Here, this will help you get over some rough spots. All we ask is that you keep trying your best to sell our products as you become more successful." We were over whelmed with gratitude and eager to produce for our benefactor.

In one form or another, several firms gave us a leg up in the early days, and believe me, we feel they're a part of the blood and bones of our organization and our loyalty to them will always remain an integral part of our selling efforts.

I'm not recommending handing out a retainer to any agency just to be nice guys. But once in a while you'll run into a rep who's just getting off the ground and barely making it, yet you can tell by his enthusiasm and ability that once he gets rolling he'll be one of your top producers. By helping him get a flying start, either by a temporary retainer or by giving him commissions on all existing business in his area, you'll have made a friend for life and you can assure yourself of his continued conscientious efforts for your company.

Are You Really Serious?

Our territory covers a lot of real estate; some towns we visit are over 600 miles away from home base. That's like going from Chicago to Pittsburgh, only our towns are much smaller and offer a much smaller sales potential than Pittsburgh. A few months ago, traveling the same territory as ours, a local rep visited one of these outposts by plane, at a cost of about $200 in plane fare, car rental, and other expenses. He brought back inquiries for three of his firms and this is what happened:

Company No. 1 quoted the customer immediately and was *shipping* parts in two weeks.

Seven weeks later, after a follow-up by the rep, Company No. 2 replied that it couldn't make the parts.

Eight weeks later, again after a follow-up, Company No. 3 said it thought it had received the inquiry but couldn't find it, so it assumed it had decided not to quote.

The inquiries sent to Companies 2 and 3 were for substantial quantities of parts, but so casual a handling of inquiries that cost $200 to obtain is more than merely a little disillusioning; it's a breach of faith. My friend says he receives phone calls periodically from the sales managers of the latter two companies, neither of whom has ever visited his territory, asking about his efforts on their behalf and voicing concern about the lack of orders. He confides that he has a ready reply for their next call. "Are you really serious?" he plans to ask.

What to Do When the Merger Comes

Go slow. If you're the surviving sales manager in the merger of two companies, the only person who has more potential problems than you is the sales manager who didn't make the cut. I'm speaking of two firms with similar product lines whose products are sold through reps, of course. All of a sudden you have two complete rep groups on your hands with two reps in each territory, and one has to go.

Naturally, your group is better than the one inherited from the merged company—or is it? How do you judge? You know your reps well, and the safest course is to retain them and drop the other company's force. But consider the inherent dangers. The other company's reps are well acquainted with many of the new customers you've gained as a result of the merger. Terminating the reps will make them unhappy, and if they've established a long-term relationship with your new customers, you're going to be exceptionally vulnerable to a loss of business to competitive lines that'll be picked up by the terminated reps. So what do you do?

As I said, go slow. After the merger you'll have to attend to numerous details to insure a smooth consolidation of sales efforts, but many of these can be delegated to subordinates. Your job is to get out into the field and personally interview your inherited reps and a representative number of their customers. Be honest about your intent; everyone knows you can't have two rep firms working for you in the same territory. Review their past history, their effectiveness, their other lines, their personnel.

If you take the time for a thorough investigation, you may find the end result surprisingly encouraging. The other company may have a star rep or two in the very area where you're the weakest. By honestly analyzing the capabilities of each rep firm and then making a decision based on your findings rather than on your emotions, you may discover that you've upgraded your rep group tremendously. By keeping the more effective reps, you'll minimize the loss of business, since the ineffective reps will have fewer opportunities to line themselves up with your better competitors. And fairness and generosity in terminating these reps will also go a long way toward bringing about a trouble-free change-over.

Want to be a Rep? Read On

The average professional football player makes $42,000 a year. My RepSurvey results show reps averaging slightly more. There's a further similarity between these two professions: in either one you make a fair amount of money or you're out of the game. Thousands of aspiring Saturday-afternoon heroes aim for big-time pro football but only a handful succeed, and injuries sometimes cut their careers short.

In the rep business, although there's no way to accurately determine the percentage of successes, it's been estimated by industry sources that only one out of nine "rookies" makes it through the first year. From that point on it takes a good number of years to reach a rewarding income level, and as in football, setbacks and failures occur that periodically thin the ranks. A top principal can be lost, an annual order can be placed elsewhere, or recession can hit one industry particularly hard.

In my view the $43,000 figure reported by my RepSurvey respondents reflects their good years. As a sales manager, I saw our reps' commissions slide from an average of $20,000 to $4,000 in a particularly poor business year, despite their best efforts. Being good businessmen they anticipated this recurring economic cycle and weathered it in good shape. To do so, however, it was necessary for them to make excellent earnings in the good years and have the discipline to put a portion aside for the poor years.

So don't put this book down and run out to become a rep without realistically assessing your chances for survival. If the urge is strong, however, the risks and dangers may be worth the rewards. It's a good life; and for the free spirit who chafes under the corporate restrictions, it's a great life. But that's a subject for another day. For the present I know that if I had it to do all over again—I would.

INDEX

AMACOM Executive Books-Paperbacks